National Cinemas and World Cinema

STUDIES IN IRISH FILM SERIES

NATIONAL CINEMAS
AND WORLD CINEMA

Studies in Irish Film 3

Kevin Rockett & John Hill
EDITORS

FOUR COURTS PRESS

Set in 10.5 on 12.5 point Ehrhardt for
FOUR COURTS PRESS LTD
7 Malpas Street, Dublin 8, Ireland
e-mail: info@four-courts-press.ie
http://www.four-courts-press.ie
and in North America by
FOUR COURTS PRESS
c/o ISBS, 920 N.E. 58th Avenue, Suite 300, Portland, OR 97213.

ISBN (13 digit) 978–1–84682–018–2 hbk
ISBN (10 digit) 1–84682–018–9

ISBN (13 digit) 978–1–84682–019–9 pbk
ISBN (10 digit) 1–84682–019–7

A catalogue record for this title
is available from the British Library.

Printed in England
by Antony Rowe Ltd, Chippenham, Wilts.

Contents

Acknowledgment

Special thanks to the Higher Education Authority's North South Programme for Collaborative Research for providing financial assistance for the Seminar series and for this publication.

Introduction

KEVIN ROCKETT & JOHN HILL

The Irish Postgraduate Film Research Seminar is a joint venture between Trinity College Dublin and the University of Ulster at Coleraine designed to promote original research in the area of Irish cinema and to encourage the training and development of researchers working in an Irish context. Since 2003, the Seminar has been supported by the Higher Education Authority's North South Programme for Collaborative Research which has made possible the provision of three postgraduate studentships, the recipients of which are included here, special training events and the publication of the Seminar proceedings. Seminars have taken place in Trinity College in 2003 and 2005, while the 2004 event was held at the University of Ulster's Portrush campus. This third volume of the *Studies in Irish Film* series contains a selection of papers presented at the 2005 Seminar.

IRELAND AND WORLD CINEMAS

One of the most rewarding developments in recent film studies has been the positioning of national cinemas in a world cinema framework. Adopting what he describes as an 'oceanic' rather than a territorial model of cinema, the distinguished film scholar Dudley Andrew suggests how cinema may operate in a transnational manner but, nevertheless, remains subject to 'local force fields'. Charting the history of successive 'new waves' in cinema, Andrew identifies a decentring of world cinema and the emergence of 'regionalist' cinemas in which the global and the local are intertwined. This then leads to a comparison between the cinemas in Ireland and Taiwan which may differ considerably in terms of political and cultural history but nonetheless share a concern to inflect 'transnational commerce' in a local direction.

The various ways in which international and local cultures intersect is a recurring concern of the essays which follow. Thus, in the second section of the volume concerned with Irish film history, Niamh McCole examines how the new international phenomenon of the cinematograph was 'customized' according to local circumstances in late nineteenth-century Ireland. Through an examination of the exhibition of films in provincial Ireland from 1896 onwards, McCole indicates how the context of reception not only had an important bearing on what was exhibited but also how films were shown and

interpreted. McCole places particular emphasis on the strong oral tradition
within Irish culture and the corresponding importance of the 'lecturer' in
mediating the meaning of films for audiences, a role that was reinforced by
the religious and political concerns of the clergy, middle-class professionals
and provincial newspapers.

Ciara Chambers' discussion is also concerned with the local reception of
international material but of a somewhat different kind. Focusing on the exhibition of newsreels during the Second World War, she indicates how Northern
and Southern Ireland had two radically different cinematic experiences during
this period. Thus, while the strict film censorship regime in neutral Southern
Ireland ensured that no representations of the war that might offend the Axis
powers were permitted, audiences in the north were fed on a diet of British
and American newsreels in which the progress of the War was the main pre-
occupation. By examining these contrasting accounts of local and international events in newsreels seen by audiences on different sides of the border,
Chambers also goes on to suggest how this may also have helped to reinforce
partition in the post-war period.

The reception of international film material in Ireland was, of course, especially significant given the relative absence of locally-produced films, particularly features, until the 1980s. Like Andrew, who considers the way in which
Peter Ormrod's *Eat the Peach* interweaves local and international concerns,
Kevin Cunnane focuses on how much recent Irish cinema has sought, partly
in pursuit of commercial success, to emulate Hollywood models of genre filmmaking. Focusing on *I Went Down* and *Divorcing Jack*, Cunnane suggests how
the adoption of Hollywood elements has led to a generically 'hybrid' cinema
which has proved only partly commercially and culturally successful. This,
Cunnane suggests, is the result of a failure to transform 'Ireland' into a fully
convincing cinematic landscape. As a result, he concludes that, while 'modern'
Irish cinema will necessarily remain 'hybrid' in character, it should avoid
dependence upon one – Hollywood – model of cinema and seek to transform,
and not just copy, the materials it borrows.

The way in which local Irish cinema inhabits the space of international
cinema, and the consequences this has for addressing the specificities of local
culture, is also a feature of Pádraic Whyte's discussion of John Sayles' *The
Secret of Roan Inish*. Attracted to Ireland for financial reasons and, as a result,
abandoning the source material's original Scottish setting, the film appears to
demonstrate how such economic forces encourage the downplaying of local
concerns in favour of the 'universal'. However, while accepting the way in
which an 'imaginary' Ireland is constructed according to the preconceptions
of an international audience, Whyte also suggests that the film self-consciously
adopts an 'idea' of Ireland in order to explore the role of myth in the modern
world. For Aileen Blaney, this interweaving of the 'concrete' and the 'uni-

versal' is also a feature of the film *H3* about the IRA hunger strikes of 1980-81. In her discussion, Blaney draws attention to the way in which the film represents the hunger strikers in an iconic Christian mode as they seek to resist the harsh prison regime through their naked bodies alone. In foregrounding this iconography, especially as it relates to Christ's suffering and the 'martyrs' of the 1916 Rising, the political import of the events is diluted as the film shifts register from a local to a more 'universal' mode of address.

The difficulties involved in representing social and political conflict is also a feature of Rashmi Sawhney's discussion of the representation of a topic all-too-familiar to the Irish viewer – sectarian violence – in two recent Indian films, *Dev* and *Mr and Mrs Iyer*. Although generically and stylistically different, Sawhney indicates how both films defy the norms of realism in pursuit of a preferred 'solution' to the conflicts they identify. Mika Ko also examines the way in which the suppressed history of the 'zainichi', or long-term Korean residents in Japan, manifests itself in Yukisada Isao's *Go!* Echoing Cunnane's observations concerning the appropriation of Hollywood conventions by cinematically-knowing Irish films, Ko indicates how the film's indebtedness to international youth style, and films such as *Trainspotting*, leads to a form of narcissistic celebration of 'oppositionality'. Thus, just as Sawhney suggests how the Indian films she discusses 'resolve' sectarian conflicts in ideologically problematic ways, so Ko indicates how the articulation of zainichi experience is ultimately subsumed within a comforting form of multiculturalism.

In demonstrating how shared concerns, such as sectarian conflict and the position of ethnic minorities, are explored in cinematically specific ways in different national contexts, such essays move in the direction of the kind of comparative study of world cinemas called for by Andrew in his opening essay. The concluding essays extend the book's international reach even further. John Waldron discusses the films of the Russian director Andrei Tarkovsky and suggests how these construct a filmic space in which the fantasy and the real, the spiritual and the ecological, merge. Alex Fisher discusses the Senegalese director Djibril Diop Mambety's *Touki Bouki*, calling for closer attention to the film's use of music. This, he suggests, complicates conventional readings of the film in terms of a straightforward conflict between tradition and modernity by indicating how the route to 'modernity' progresses in culturally specific – and contradictory – ways. In doing so, he also provides further evidence of the ways in which local cinemas appropriate and re-articulate imported cultural repertoires. Finally, Liz Greene adds to Fisher's call for more attention to film music with a demand for more consideration of film sound. Focusing on the pioneering work of sound designer Alan Splet, in collaboration with the director David Lynch, she identifies the complex play between synchronous and asynchronous sound to be found in a film such as *Blue Velvet*.

The three volumes that now constitute the *Studies in Irish Film* series have brought together a wide range of writers whose topics have explored hitherto under-explored aspects of Irish and world cinemas. Many of the twenty-five different contributors have already moved on from research to teaching and other professional activities, and are now imparting to new students the knowledge gained and research skills acquired during their student careers. We wish them, and those who are following in their wake, well.

Part 1: Mapping World Cinema

Islands in the sea of cinema[1]

DUDLEY ANDREW

In the past decade, just as a string of excellent books came along to lay out the contours of Irish cinema with impressive detail, the market value of 'national cinemas' took a plunge everywhere. Today, even while most curricula include courses in French, Japanese, German, Chinese, and, yes, Irish Cinema, more and more film scholars repudiate this territorial model in their written work, replacing it with one or another 'world systems' model. One variant would shift focus from territories to the sea that unites them and across which films and discourse travel. Between these extremes of territory (nation) and ocean (globe), I want to insert an intermediate concept, 'regional cinema,' in order to acknowledge the way that today (and I believe always) cinema operates in a transnational manner, subject of course to local force fields. Thus, John Hill, Martin McLoone and Paul Hainsworth were prescient when, in advance of the spate of Irish National Cinema books, and before the rush to abstract global overviews, they edited the aptly titled: *Border Crossing: film in Ireland, Britain and Europe* (1994).

Shifting from a territorial toward an oceanic model encourages a reassessment of the idea of 'new waves' in world cinema. Whereas the original waves of the 1960s occurred as palace revolutions within such hide-bound national cinemas as that of France, Japan, the USSR, Brazil, and Czechoslovakia, a second set of waves in the 1980s should be seen first as a regional phenomenon, where strong films from various places in Africa and along the Pacific Rim crashed against the lighthouses of film festivals. A third set of waves has been touted by festivals since 1995 in a gesture that is genuinely global rather than international; this time it seems that the festivals – and there are hundreds of them – effectively administer fashion, by programming and even instigating world trends and stylistic difference like curators at high-profile museums who commission indigenous art. Can a genuine wave emerge when DVDs and the internet have put all styles on display everywhere on the globe and when films seem made with festivals in mind? Is there anything outside the system that can surprise us?

The 'us' in my last sentence refers to western cinephiles who relish surprise. I would like to put 'us' in our place in the history of world cinema by

1 This paper was developed for the conference at Trinity College Dublin in April 2005 and will be the germ of an expanded contribution to Kathleen Newman and Natasa Durovicova (eds), *Transnational cinema* (London, 2006).

15

examining the place of the Pacific Rim in the sixty years since festivals promised to promote universal humanism through the polylogue of films. In a larger survey I would focus on three different functions of festivals that effectively responded to those three different sets of 'new waves,' each of which involved Asian cinema. Here I will race through the first two such periods (World War II to 1968 and 1982–93) to show, first, that each depended on the idea of a 'different cinema' produced somewhere in Asia, and, second, to suggest how the idea of 'Asian cinema' differed in the two cases.

II

Has there ever been a more stunning and unexpected festival triumph than that of *Rashomon* at Venice in 1951? This was the first film from beyond Europe and North America to compete since the festival's founding in 1932. Compared to Olivier's *Hamlet* or Clouzot's *Manon* (the previous years' winners), *Rashomon* looked muscular, a film that knew of what cinema was capable. Only Bresson's *Journal d'un curé de compagne* received comparable attention that year, and for much the same reason, I would argue. Venice became the breeding ground of a series of Japanese masterworks, with Mizoguchi's *Saikaku ichidai onna* scoring there in 1952, *Ugetsu* taking the Silver Lion in 1953 and *Sansho Dayu* splitting that Lion with Kurosawa's *Seven Samurai* in 1954. Cannes gave its top prize in 1953 to Kinugasa's *Gate of Hell*.

The Japanese had moved cinema forward by merging what Paul Willemen calls archaic and modernist forms of enunciation.[2] Or, to take the formulation both Willemen and I have adopted from Franco Moretti and Fredric Jameson, 'in cultures that belong to the periphery of the literary system, the modern novel first arises not as an autonomous development but as a compromise between a western formal influence (usually French or English) and local materials'.[3] Moretti understands that local material is more than sheer stuff to be shoved into forms of narrative borrowed from advanced literary cultures.[4] It includes indigenous traditions of storytelling and pictorial representation. This process operates visibly in West African films that so frequently include oral storytellers on screen. Invariably financed by European agencies, these films, ostensibly made for African spectators, are meant to be overheard by consumers of art cinema fascinated by the look and sound of such archaic fabulation. The same formula, wherein local narration accords with cosmopolitan taste for difference, may well stand behind the critical successes of key Taiwanese and Irish films that will concern us when we reach the situation of 'second waves'.

2 Paul Willemen, 'For a comparative film studies', *Inter-Asia Cultural Studies*, 6:1 (2005), p. 103.
3 Franco Moretti, 'Conjectures on world literature,' *New Left Review*, 1 (Jan.–Feb. 2000), p. 58.
4 Moretti, 'Conjectures,' esp. fn 25 relating to African oral traditions.

Keeping the incredible Japanese successes of the 1950s in view, the Jameson-Moretti law would emphasize their local subject matter. All of them are *jidei-geki*, that is, period dramas made with special fervour following the five-year injunction on the genre imposed by the American Occupiers. But Kurosawa and Mizoguchi did not simply pour their ancient tales into borrowed western moulds; indeed it was *Rashomon's* innovative fabulation that caused the shock at Venice and that still attracts attention. The same is true, I could argue in detail, for the Mizoguchi films. In Europe *Ugetsu Monogatari* bore the evocative title *Conte de la lune vague après la pluie*, readying its foreign audience for the artful telling of an otherworldly fable. And when that tale concludes with the point of view of a ghost, western audiences were dumbfounded. How did Mizoguchi slip so unnoticeably from one state of being to another, enticing us to sympathize with the feelings of a ghost who then evaporates when dawn appears under the crack of a doorway? Actually, European audiences ought to have been prepared, since one section of *Rashomon*, screened two years earlier, had been narrated by a ghost through a 'medium' (after the medium herself had been conjured up by the men recounting the crime and trial under the Rashomon Gate in that dreadful downpour). Both prize-winning films, then, dipped deep into the past where troubling stories are told by liminal beings who point towards a still murkier past. Even later fifties' works by European fabulists like Bergman and Fellini appear not nearly so subtle in comparison.

The strength of Japanese cinema in the 1950s augured the displacement of cinematic power from the West and toward Asia, something that would be officially recognized only after 1980. In the 1950s, and despite the French retreat from Indo-China after Dien-Bien-Phu, even those Europeans proud of their liberal 'international perspective' assumed that Paris was the Wall Street where cinematic values traded and were in some sense safeguarded. When *Cahiers du Cinéma* championed Mizoguchi, it was to recruit him for a French revolution in cinema which, like that original French Revolution of 1789, was thought to be both national and universal. In 1960, celebrating the first birthday of the New Wave, *Cahiers'* 'ten best' list put Mizoguchi's *Sansho Dayu* at the summit, after which came Godard's *Breathless*, Truffaut's *Shoot the Piano Player* and Chabrol's *Les Bonnes Femmes*. The revelation of *Sansho* at Venice six years earlier had at last been vindicated by a successful Parisian distribution; and so the New Wave critics-turned-cinéastes deliberately but proudly set their own accomplishments beneath it. Jacques Rivette had already declared this affinity, claiming that Mizoguchi spoke not Japanese but rather the only language filmmakers should speak, 'the universal language of *mise-en-scène*', which after all is a French term that the rest of the cinema world has come to adopt.[5]

5 Jacques Rivette, 'Mizoguchi, vu d'ici', *Cahiers du Cinéma* 81 (March 1958). Translated in Jim Hillier (ed.), *Cahiers du Cinéma: the 1950s* (Cambridge, 1985), p. 264.

In my BFI-Classics monograph on *Sansho Dayu*, I argue that this film achieved centrality (became a classic) only by standing deliberately at the periphery: a mother's voice wafted to her children from atop a windswept palisade on the Western isle of Sado, the children catching from her the spirit of family unity as a Buddhist imperative. Mercy and grace do not emerge in the centre of civilization, whether conceived of as Kyoto in the eleventh century or as Paris and Hollywood in 1954; instead grace comes unexpectedly from across the water. Mizoguchi sent his great tragedy from the periphery and from the past to disturb the conscience of modern Japan. Venice overheard it as a voice from the East, from 'Mizoguchi the Master',[6] resonating with the eerie sonority of a past inaccessible at the time to Western film aesthetics. Such an ancient voice could be felt to emanate from the father's death mask in *Ugetsu*, and to be passed along in the flashbacks at the outset of *Sansho* that are mystically shared by mother and son.

Thus it was the *form* of Mizoguchi's films, not their local *material*, which astounded the French. From the Venice festival of 1953 – and in a collection edited by Bazin – a critic wrote of the utterly new feeling conveyed by *Ugetsu* with its 'temporal schema utterly distinct from Western dramatics'.[7] Drawing on archaic traditions as distant from the European festivals as could be, Japan renewed the modern art of cinema. Bound together through federations of festivals and ciné-clubs, modern cinema felt itself enriched by developments on the other side of the globe. But make no mistake, the critics and cinephiles who followed such things did so in the pages of Paris' *Cahiers du Cinéma* (or London's *Sight and Sound*, or the annual catalogues from Cannes, Venice, Locarno, and Berlin); that is, from the heart of Europe.[8]

Should we then take the nouvelle vague to be a *nouvelle onde*, a shortwave spreading out from a source atop the Eiffel Tower to proclaim the French revolution in cinema? Viewers in selected capitals certainly tuned in to its frequency. But, no; the oceanographic rather than the broadcast metaphor seems far more apposite for cinema. After all, distribution patterns of export, subtitling, and dubbing, as well as the migration of actors, directors, and cinematographers, help account for the logic of stylistic change in the more mobile years following World War II. In fact in the 1950s, most films and directors

6 It was under this rubric that the last retrospective of Mizoguchi's films made its way around Europe and North America in the 1990s. 7 In André Bazin, *Cinéma 53 à travers le monde* (Paris, 1954), p. 174. 8 As Robert Young argues, the humiliation of France's reduced political scope after Dien-Bien Phu begins with a literal re-orientation of cultural strength, evident, for instance, in Jean-Paul Sartre's 1948 essay about Negritude called 'Black Orpheus'. Whereas Europe, assuming that the West would remain the Wall Street of international culture, had always been pleased to display the world's cultural achievements (and the first film festivals persisted in just this mission), it would now have to consider a world whose values and future were completely out of its rule. Yet it refused to recognize this for many years. See Young, Introduction to *White mythologies: writing history and the West* (London, 1990).

moved around by ship. I imagine this of Yasuzo Masamura, who, after accompanying Mizoguchi to Venice for one of the films on which he worked as assistant, stayed on in Italy at the Centro Sperimentale. Intoxicated by the ambience of a developing European youth culture, he criticized Mizoguchi for his old-fashioned aestheticism. Masamura inspired Oshima, Imamura, and Yoshida, all of whom declared themselves finished with the past and ready to give voice to the resentful youth of their own generation. Characters in the films of all four directors spout or mumble shocking colloquialisms in films that were immediately publicized as the 'Japanese New Wave'. This swift adoption of the term validates the aptness of a 'fluid' metaphor, for the French movement really did have consequences in Japan, which then may have washed back to affect the radical Brazilian *cinema nôvo*, since that country always imported Shochiku films from Tokyo. In brief, the first set of new waves were national uprisings before becoming international causes. For instance, throughout the 1950s the *Cahiers du Cinéma* critics flooded French cultural journals in order to submerge a national system called the 'Cinéma de Qualité' and so to establish freer conditions that would allow new blood and new films to emerge. Their Japanese, Brazilian, German, and East Europeans confrères monitored and applauded this Parisian takeover (especially at festivals) and followed suit, each fighting its own very different cultural hegemony in what was at best a federation of separate internal revolts.

III

The heady days of student revolution, of new cinema, and of European arrogance were brutally undercut by the political defeats of 1968. The art film lost its glamour and art theatres began a decline from which they never recovered. What about film festivals? Whether out of clairvoyance or an instinct for survival, festivals moved toward becoming 'world' rather than 'international' events. The difference is key. Cannes inaugurated the 'Quinzaine de Réalisiteurs' and 'Un Certain Regard' so as to expose a greater variety of films coming from no matter where. On the American continent, Toronto and Montreal ('Festival du cinéma du monde') sprang to life in 1975, soon showing more than 300 films annually, very few coming from the U.S. Hong Kong's great festival also opened in 1975, and FESPACO in Burkina Faso kept the new African cinema in view every other year.

Sucked into the vacuum felt at festivals by the retreat of the European art cinema came films from places never before thought of as cinematically interesting or viable: places like Mainland China, Senegal, Mali, Yugoslavia, Ireland, Taiwan, and Iran. Distinct from the new waves of the 1960s in their provenance, they also functioned in a greatly changed international system. Besides the demise of the European art film, one must calculate the effects of the new economics of Hollywood distribution in the wake of *Star Wars* (1977) as well as the predicted impact of Betamax and VHS tapes. Such immense meteorological pressures circulated everywhere when the next set of new waves began to roll from ocean to ocean and coastline to coastline in the 1980s.

At the crest of those waves one always finds visionary auteurs whose works opened up cinematic public spheres where none had existed before, challenging the official discourse of state media on the one side and the global discourse of Hollywood on the other. Audiences in Yugoslavia could recognize within Emir Kusturica's dynamic mobile frame the mass of disparate languages, religions, classes, as well as the disputed pasts that made the Balkans the pressure cooker it was. In Mali and Burkina Faso, Souleymane Cissé and Gaston Kaboré abandoned the soviet cinema models of the immediate postcolonial moment for an original cultural critique that called on oral and pre-colonial sources. Yugoslavia and West Africa both retain more than the vestiges of oral culture; the same has been said of Ireland, of course, particularly when set beside England: the lyric poem, the ironic anecdote, the pub banter is thrown in the face of thick Victorian novels and multi-volume histories coming out of London. Thus, I would say that second wave films, oral and 'minor,' are meant to be overheard by an art cinema audience. Their discourse is bi-lingual, in Homi Bhabha's sense, mimicking while adapting or undermining proper mise-en-scène and montage. The Romany music and language in *Time of the Gypsies* (1988) allowed Kusturica to celebrate an impure and undervalued aesthetic operating in his own Bosnian situation. Kusturica, you may know, is a founder of the 'No Smoking Orchestra' with its *unza unza* motifs carrying gypsy wildness into all his films. In beleaguered places perhaps cinema stands closer to music than to fiction: ever since *Djeli* (1982), a host of African films open with a griot playing a stringed instrument and intoning the film as a tale. As for the urban films of Africa, from the *La Vie est Belle* (1987) to *Quartier Mozart* (1992) with its MTV motifs, these I take to be versions of afropop. Similarly, whatever the 'voice' of Irish cinema may be, should it not be heard as a variant of English, a 'regionalism,' as it were?

In their desire to clear a space of representation, to claim or reclaim their territory and their past, and to offer these images to a world waiting for a grounded glimpse of what has been an absent or imaginary place, these new waves of the 1980s developed a 'critical regionalism'. I take up this charged term elaborated by Cheryl Herr in relation to Ireland, because it names a practice of representation that, while refusing the facile temptations of rooted cultural nationalism, holds out against the 'administered culture' of globalization.[9] Between nation and globe one can glimpse unofficial third spaces, interstitial regions that recognize their distinctiveness without denying their connectedness to the outside. In the 1980s such interstitial spaces found themselves physi-

9 Cheryl Herr, *Critical regionalism and cultural studies* (Gainesville, 1996), 'Introduction'.

cally located at film festivals where directors and producers encouraged one another, formulated projects, looked for distribution deals, and above all registered the existence of films that otherwise would have been invisible. We may distinguish this 1980s regionalism from the new waves of the 1960s which effectively stood out as so many separate cinematic bohemias set within nation-states (by which they were sometimes fostered). From their artistic ghetto, for example, Czechoslovakian filmmakers may have recognized a neighbouring ghetto in Hungary, but did they sense their affinity to Cuban or Japanese auteurs? Film festivals in the 1960s exhibited new works, but they did not yet constitute a transnational space as they would in the 1980s when they sent scouts into the field to ferret out work distinctive of regions that may not have been previously represented. After Global Hollywood took over so much exhibition space on the continent, European critics traveled to Africa and Asia, looking for a renewal of an art form that could no longer be expected to come routinely from Euro – or at least from the heart of Europe. They had to travel to take account of what had become a completely decentred world art form.

If these critics had only looked to the edge of their own continent, they would have noticed in Ireland a developing 'Critical Regionalist' cinema that bears comparison with comparable efforts screened at festivals from 'no matter where'. To explore the notion of a decentred world cinema, let's compare the region surrounding Ireland to one surrounding an island at its near antipodes, Taiwan. What attracts me to this curious comparison is that neither island figured in discussions of cinema until the 1980s.[10] A look at these regions can therefore help distill the forces involved in a transnational approach to World cinema.

IV

On first blush, the uncanny resemblance of the Irish cinema situation to Taiwan's helps frame and measure both. These islands share a history of questioned national status; both have suffered gruesome histories of colonialism and internal political division. Ireland may be more the size of Hong Kong in population, but it approximates Taiwan's demographic configuration, with villages (some speaking an indigenous language) being sucked into urban modernity. The south/north tension in Taiwan rotates ninety degrees to align with the west/east divide that has shaped Irish self-representation (W.B. Yeats versus James Joyce, if you will).

If you squint at the globe as at the stars, you can recognize equivalent constellations of power that govern the fortune of each island's political economy and culture. China plays for Taiwan the substantial role of the USA in

---

10 Evidently island cultures occasion massive scholarship. The number of strong books on Taiwan's cinema published recently in English surpasses those on Irish cinema.

Irish history, since these huge land masses exert incalculable gravitational pull
to the West. Japan would be equivalent, then, to England as one-time colo-
nizers, vestiges of whose architecture, language, and food remain – along with
great hostility. Finally both islands have negotiated with an outside power to
give them political and economic ballast. Ireland has been resurrected by the
European Union through whose financial and cultural intercession it has
emerged proudly as 'the Celtic Tiger'. To be suddenly positioned on the
superhighway of the global economy, however, threatens Ireland's cultural distinctiveness. Cannot the same thing be said of Taiwan's use (and fear) of
America's economic partnership? American economic investment may have
helped Taiwan lever its independence years back, but the island has also served
as the fulcrum when America leaned its political muscle on Asia. Unlike the
European Union, the USA has never cared about Taiwan's cultural identity.
Yet Taiwan, like Ireland, can play the caroms on this international pool table
in such a way as to travel a course partly of its own choosing. The cinema is
a key measurement of that course; it is also one of the brightest billiard balls
on the table, being struck directly time and again.

   If today we can identify some of the ocean currents and warm fronts that
affected filmmaking conditions in a given region, no weather satellite view was
available to those on the ground when in 1982–83 Neil Jordan and Edward
Yang were making their first features. When Hou Hsiao-Hsien made *Boys
from Fengkuei* (1983) and *Sandwich Man* (1983), he worked not according to
some grand aesthetic plan but rather by instinct, claiming he was conscious
neither of Ozu nor of the French New Wave.[11] He was just glad to burst
through the tiny opening of encouragement held out, for whatever reasons,
by prescient policies formulated by new officials at the Central Motion Picture
Company. Drawing inspiration from recent 'neorealist' fiction, he set out to
record and broadcast a chorus of voices that had not before been heard in
Taiwanese motion pictures, and to project on the screen not just long repressed
images but a cognitive map oriented to the Taipei meridian. Ultimately he
helped to liberate a cinematographic culture that had been strait-jacketed in
an increasingly irrelevant studio system and to bring back an audience hijacked
by foreign distribution keyed to Hollywood.

   At the outset of the 1980s things were worse for Irish filmmaking, since
there was not even a moribund system to renew. Aspiring filmmakers started
practically from scratch, with scant hope of carving out space in a market given
over entirely to global distributors, purveying primarily Hollywood fare. But,
as in Taiwan, short films fueled ambitions, as experiments in local documentary and fiction found a strong following. With the precedent of Bob Quinn's
Poitín (1978) and with a certain amount of patronage (Channel 4 in Britain

11 James Udden, 'The strange apprenticeship of Hou Hsiao-Hsien', *Modern Chinese Literature and
Culture* 15:1 (2003), p. 140.

plus a stuttering state effort), independent feature films got underway at the rate of a couple per year. Neil Jordan's *Angel* (1982) was the first to gain attention beyond the island. Notably, it played in the Malaysian festival of 1984, just as at least one Chinese film would be part of the Cork festival each year from 1984 on.

Especially because Anglophone, Ireland has always been a pawn in the global media game. It is an important exhibition outlet for Hollywood (largest per capita box office in Europe if one discounts Iceland) and a site for outsourced projects like *Braveheart* and *King Arthur*. As happens everywhere, Ireland has offered up its history, geography and literature in a rather official bid for international esteem or nostalgia (*Fools of Fortune* [1990], *Far and Away* [1992], *Dancing at Lughnasa* [1998]). Nevertheless, as the number of productions grew to a dependable number in the early 1990s, unofficial films could sprout in unlikely regions (the west, the north, the city suburbs), producing what Irish critics are fond of calling 'rooted cosmopolitanism'. The best of these remain inveterately local (in verbal language, allusions, geography, and acting) while putting themselves smartly in touch with a larger world that may or may not be directly referenced. The size of that world is elastic, stretching to the demands or possibilities inherent in the film's subject matter and production. Irish films haven't needed to see themselves automatically in relation either to the realities of Hollywood or to some sublime idea of global media. Neither have they often retreated to their private cultural heritage (though a couple of fawning films come out every year). Irish cineastes have been free to imagine variable spatial dimensions, looking out to a region that sometimes includes Britain (*The Crying Game* [1992]), Scandinavia (*The Disappearance of Finbar* [1996]), Europe (*Guiltrip* [1995]), Japan (*Eat the Peach* [1986]) or the USA (*The Commitments* [1991]).

But I don't mean to retrace the root and branch structure of two sapling national cinemas; quite the opposite. Specific conditions of production and exhibition catalyzed ingenious efforts to bring local issues strikingly to the screen on these two islands, but it was understood that survival as well as success required looking offshore as well. In 1986, after a government backlash against this upstart cinema movement, Taiwanese film activists drew up a manifesto based on the Oberhausen prototype that had kick-started the New German Cinema back in 1962.[12] To gain the sympathy of local critics and audiences, they determined to take a detour through foreign festivals. Hou Hsiou-Hsien vindicated this strategy in 1989, when his difficult and taxing masterpiece, *A City of Sadness*, after returning with the Silver Lion from Venice, became the single biggest box-office success to date in Taiwan. The same year Jim Sheridan's *My Left Foot* (1989) attracted a huge home audience proud of

12 Peggy Chiao, roundtable on Taiwan distribution problems, Yale University conference 'Double Vision', October 2003.

the attention lavished on it by the New York Film Critics, the Oscars, the judges at the Montreal festival and elsewhere.

To account for the varying ratio of national to world perspective adopted by key Irish filmmakers I have coined the term 'demi-emigration'.[13] Ever since James Joyce composed *Dubliners* abroad, writers and filmmakers have had to negotiate the watery space between Ireland and two continents. The same I sense is true in Taiwan, so that I'm tempted to line up key directors by what they take from home and from various places abroad as they go about the work of what Fredric Jameson has called 'cognitive mapping' for an audience that is never strictly local.

In a talk at Yale's Taiwan film conference in 2003, Jameson neatly graphed the key directions taken. While Hou Hsiao-Hsien sliced into the island's past, reading its layers diachronically like an archeologist, Edward Yang has taken synchronic slices. From *That Day on the Beach* (1983) to *YiYi/A One and a Two* ... (1999), Jameson finds Yang to represent the 'synchronous Monadic Simultaneity' that he defined in his formidable discussion of *Terroriser* (1986).[14] Yang pursues a modernist, even international aesthetic, inflected by his experience in the USA and his interest in Japan. This would put him in the line of James Joyce, representing urban modernity. His screen stretches to hold in a single view a number of perspectives, private and social, intimate aspirations and family rituals ... all these atop the hard realities of glass and metal that make up Taipei. Let's pluralize the title of his 1985 film *Taipei Story* so as to see his corpus as related short fictions akin to *Dubliners*. In his largest works, *Yi Yi* and *Terroriser*, the virtuoso intertwining of contradictory impulses and pressures felt in urban life recalls *Ulysses* and its literary progeny.

To keep the Irish analogy alive, Hou Hsiao-Hsien in his initial phase, mined his country's past, its rural values, its languages and its sufferings rather in the manner of W.B. Yeats during the Irish Literary Revival. Of course Yeats came from privileged Anglican stock that had colonized the west of the country. Yet it is he who rooted Ireland to the past (while Joyce, in the sociological majority- catholic, urban, of a lower class – bolted from the country to join an international artistic company). Similarly, of all Taiwanese it is Hou – belonging to the 1948 Mainland arrivistes – who has brought the island's memories to screen. Hou recently reiterated Yeats-like sentiments about 'a unique Taiwanese creative consciousness, which is closely related to this earth we grow on and our whole cultural background'.[15] In excavating Taiwan's layered pasts, his films discover and are pierced by shards protruding both from the Japanese era and, after their defeat, from the brutal era of Chiang Kai-

13 Dudley Andrew, 'The theater of Irish Cinema', *Yale Journal of Criticism*, 15:1 (2002), pp 23–58. 14 Fredric Jameson, 'Remapping Tapei', in *The geopolitical aesthetic: cinema and space in the world system* (Bloomington, 1992). 15 Hou Hsiao-Hsien, 'In search of new genres and directions for Asian cinema', *Rouge*, 1 (2003).

Chek's takeover. Hou makes one listen for muffled, sometimes overlapping voices speaking various languages. His frames so often give onto other frames, each holding a moment that is modified by something that returns from the past. The compositions tunnel from the foreground through doorways and down corridors, keeping multiple dramatic planes in view and with it a tension between past and present, here and elsewhere. Hou's Taiwan is an island-scape that can only be understood as marked by the passage of people to and from, China, Hong Kong and especially Japan. His latest films make this strikingly clear. *Millennium Mambo* (2001) concludes in Japan, *Café Lumière* (2003), commissioned by Japan and set there, concerns a Japanese/Taiwanese historical figure, and the middle story in *Three Times* (2005) is set in 1911 with plenty of references not just to the Japanese occupation but to Tokyo which the protagonist visits.

Updating his discussion of the Taiwanese new wave, Jameson recently opposed Ang Lee to Tsai Ming-Liang, the maximizer to the minimalist. Ang Lee like Edward Yang employs an expansive screen to spread his characters and their conflicting feelings out. Using techniques acquired in the USA, he progressively inflates domestic situations (genre scenes) until they culminate in an image of a social totality, which visibly wavers on the screen. *Eat Drink Man Woman* (1994) provided Ang Lee with a Taiwanese subject and feeling which he could treat with confidence, before tackling what he takes to be a related project, *Sense and Sensibility* (1996). Similarly, *Crouching Tiger, Hidden Dragon* (2000) takes its start in the King Hu martial arts films that first put Taiwan on the international cinema map; Ang Lee literally inflates the genre until it stretches the screen to reach every corner of China. Taiwan provides Ang Lee with material he knows how to turn into international capital, making him far more versatile than, say, the fully Americanized Wayne Wang. Lee, the demi-emigrant, is an Asian-American living in the suburbs of New York, yet attached sentimentally and culturally – that is, by genre – to Taiwan. Yet Ang Lee's Taiwan was always already transnational. As Darrell Davis and Emilie Yeh have demonstrated, *Eat Drink Man Woman* replays a fabulously popular film of the late 1950s, *Our Sister Hedy*, that also treats the tribulations of four girls devoted to their widowed father.[16] Shot in Hong Kong, *Heddy* responded to the *Little Women* (Louisa May Alcott) craze that swept Taiwan after the Korean war. Thus an Asian-American director goes to Taiwan to remake a Hong Kong film that is based on a classic American novel. Are his films truly Taiwanese? What difference does that make, if the island gives him both the perspective and the lift for which he is justly praised. *Eat Drink* and *Crouching Tiger* both conclude on buoyant expressions of free flight, with characters released from constricting pressures. No doubt Ang Lee has

16 Emilie Yueh-Yu Yeh and Darrell Davis, *Taiwan film directors: a treasure island* (New York, 2005), pp 211–14.

experienced just this sense of release each time he boards a plane heading either way across the Pacific. From such a height, Taipei's complexity, indeed the complexities of one's own life, appear in view and all at once, the advantage of an island-scape.[17]

Tsai Ming-Liang, on the other hand, takes Taipei apart in *The Hole* (1998), in *The Skywalk Is Gone* (2002), and in *Good-Bye Dragon Inn* (2003). Born in Malaysia, itinerant in his personal life, and attached to the international art scene, he declares himself homeless,[18] yet his films bank on the texture of life in Taipei and on its crumbling architecture. That city's perpetual transformation make it a space of demolition, which Tsai figures as a 'hole,' the title of a film in which two very isolated characters living one atop the other in an apartment complex, are barely connected through an aperture drilled into the man's floor. Tsai's films are indeed apertures, or tunnels, that lead to the dead ends of box-like apartments and to the funeral boxes in mausoleums. With space collapsing, characters are left to wait and to imagine. 'What Time is it There?' ask the characters in another of his thematically titled films (one from Paris, the other from Taipei). To conceive, to make, and to exhibit his films, Tsai needs Taiwan yet needs to leave it. As with Ang Lee, only the simultaneous presence of the *here* and of the *elsewhere* permits the gestures of his films: Ang Lee's leap into a liberating space is equivalent to Tsai's being drawn down into confinement with space narrowing all around.

Following Jameson's mission to map the cinematic potential within the Taiwanese cinema by looking at the tendencies of its strongest filmmakers, we might say that, due perhaps to their years living in the USA, Ang Lee and Edward Yang express themselves on *screen*, in broad space. By contrast, Hou Hsiao-Hsien (especially in the 1980s) and Tsai Ming-Liang drill into their subjects using a constricted frame, sometimes narrowing it to the size of an *aperture*. Aperture and screen: every film exists as the passage of light from the first to the second. Apertures and screens form a single image-forming system. The friction that signals the work accomplished in Taiwanese films can be felt both at the point of aperture (in the representation of temporality by Hou Hsiao-Hsien and Tsai Ming-Liang) and on the screen (the quest to represent social spaces in the work of Edward Yang and Ang Lee). Struggling to represent Taiwanese experience, they bring a world just beyond the screen into appearance. Consider the island itself as aperture giving onto the region or as a screen where the region can with difficulty be made out and, in the large sense of the word, comprehended. Such an effort to bring the offscreen into the picture, contrasts with the effortlessness of global films, so many of

17 A recent concept in geography and archeology, 'islandscape' takes in the landmass of an island together with surrounding waters and other lands. See for instance Cyprian Broodbank, *An island archaeology of the early cyclades* (Cambridge, 2000), esp. chap. 8.   18 Tsai Ming-Liang, interview with the author, 3 Oct. 2003, New Haven, CT.

them made in nearby Hong Kong. Released from the encumbrances of geography and history, global films are released like balloons into the atmosphere where they offer the smooth ride of entertainment. In Taiwan, however, the passage between aperture and screen is always difficult, but difficulty is also what anchors the New Taiwanese cinema to experience; this is a weighty cinema, a complex cinema, where the effortless routine of genres scarcely applies.

V

Two paradigmatic images serve as my conclusion, both from 1986, the year when unmistakably a new set of waves was on the horizon. The first, from the opening of Hou Hsiou-Hsien's *Dust in the Wind* (1986), takes us from aperture to screen. After long moments of absolute darkness a tiny spot is visible, growing and growing until we burst from a tunnel on a slow train into a verdant landscape of hills and into the social time of historical memory. A couple gets off at a forlorn village station, then saunter down a country road conversing, the man with a bag of rice on his shoulder. All of a sudden they stop short, noticing something ahead of them. A reverse shot shows a nondescript area at the edge of town where a huge sheet, billowing slightly, is being strung up by ropes to hang suspended in the air. 'It's a screen', the man says. 'They'll be showing a film tonight'. The train tracks go off to the left of the screen and mountains rise steep behind it.[19] The images to follow, comprising the rest of *Dust in the Wind* and, by extension, all future Taiwanese films, will take their place on such a screen, situated here in the depths of the country. From the aperture of the tunnel into the centre of the island, we are arrested by this blank screen, which forms another aperture giving onto the land that surrounds it. Taiwanese cinema promises to contribute to the islandscape from a point within it.

Simultaneously, but on the other side of the globe, another figure of cinema was being erected in the centre of yet another island: the 'wall of death' amusement attraction in Peter Ormrod's *Eat the Peach*. This ungainly cylinder, a silo sitting atop a seemingly endless field of peat, stands out from its surroundings like a theatre. 'This wooden O, this cockpit' is there to launch the imagination of those who come to watch the motorcyclists gain speed to climb the walls. Like this ridiculous contraption, *Eat the Peach* and a raft of Irish films to follow, appears jerry-rigged and awkward. But it manages to mimic, in its self-deprecating manner, the industries of entertainment (VCRs from Japan, films from Hollywood), while making something out of the infertile

19 Chris Berry and Feii Lu (eds), *Island on the edge: Taiwan New Cinema and after* (Hong Kong, 2005).

nothing of this bog of a land. Whatever its qualities, and however judged, *Eat the Peach* has constructed a literal image of rooted cosmopolitanism at the gutsy outset of the new Irish cinema. For the next ten years, right up to the proud and properly financed *Michael Collins*, ragtag but imaginative productions would carve out a space – the cylinder transformed into public sphere – that, while set within the island, kept separate from the State. Attentive to what is both larger and smaller than the Republic (represented in *Eat the Peach* by the slimy politician as well as by television), Irish cinema of the 1980s and early 1990s emerged as critical regionalist in all senses of that term.

What could be left of this robust sensibility in the twentieth century, when DVDs and the internet have so hastened the entropy of genuine cultural difference and caustic aesthetic friction? Like Celtic music, Irish cinema inevitably plays into a sophisticated and all-embracing global distribution market. But if contrariness and idiosyncrasy are still to be found, I would look for it on craggy islandscapes, like Ireland and Taiwan, where geography retards the smooth flow of people, products, ideas, money, and images. Full participants in the global system, these island cultures are nevertheless able to exact a 'value added' tax to the accelerating transnational commerce. In cinema this amounts to the irreducible evidence of a local sensibility (habits, references, gestures, and concerns) tied to struggles of social history that, despite the digitally cleansed appearance of movies everywhere, cannot and must not be forgotten or aestheticized.

Part 2: Cinema in Ireland

The cinematograph in provincial Ireland 1896–1906: exhibition and reception

NIAMH McCOLE

This essay offers a historical survey of the arrival of the cinematograph in provincial Ireland from 1896 onwards. Proceeding by means of an analysis of newspaper reviews, I trace its exhibition and reception in the provinces during the first ten years of its history and indicate the ways in which the new medium was appropriated within provincial Ireland. The paper suggests that, rather than bringing with it an unvarying set of meanings and practices to be replicated regardless of temporal or geographic location, the cinematograph in provincial Ireland was customized according to a repertoire of cultural values that was both implicitly mobilized by viewers and explicitly championed by organizations such as the Gaelic League and the clergy.

I will look at the prevailing cultural and political forces in nineteenth-century Ireland which both created and shaped the attitudes and expectations of cinematograph audiences. Five key factors emerge as particularly significant. The first involves the exhibition context, the deportment of audiences and their sense of participation and communality. The second concerns the marked ambivalence of audiences to the quality and 'authenticity' of cinematograph images while the third refers to the strong preference of audiences for the exhibition of films featuring local people, places and events. The fourth factor concerns a bias in favour of the 'oral' qualities of entertainment at the expense of the visual while the fifth deals with the influence of, and direct interventions by, the clergy and cultural revivalists.

EXHIBITION: THE SOCIAL AUDIENCE

The exhibition context during the period in question fostered a fundamentally different conception of audience membership and spectatorship to that which we know today. It is clear from provincial Irish press reports during the period in question that film-spectator relations were characterized by both the visibility of audience members and by a social dimension. Many reviews begin by listing the names of individuals in attendance, often with their addresses and occupations supplied. Notable absences are also included and explained. Thus, a report (in the *Clonmel Chronicle*) that '[t]he Rev. Wm. Phelan, P.P., owing to

31

a slight indisposition, was unable to attend'[1] a particular cinematograph exhibition indicates a knowledge on the part of individuals that their presence, or indeed absence, was likely to be noted. Moreover, unlike the 'fixed and isolated observer' of classical cinema, it was common for audience members to exercise mobility during a performance. The reviewer of the *Sligo Champion*, for example, objected to the suggestion that a Press Box should be provided for reviewers on the grounds that reviewers 'might want to go out "to see a man" and if they were boxed up they could not do so'. 'It is better under present circumstances', he continued, 'to give certain critics the run of the front seats to go in and out as their inclination or thirstiness dictates'.[2]

The circumstances of exhibition were clearly crucial to the forging of the audience's sense of itself as an audience. The viewing situation permitted the audience present to be addressed as a collective entity. The range and organization of ancillary entertainment features, such as the singing of popular songs (sometimes illustrated by lantern views in which the chorus lyrics were projected on screen), dancing and recitations, established a strong connection between the screen and the physical space of the theatre and encouraged audience participation. Provincial Irish audiences, therefore, conceived of themselves as a public gathering, an active force not merely witnessing but participating in the performance. The social atmosphere of cinematograph exhibitions allowed for their active involvement, clearly signalled in the reviews by the inclusion of accounts of their appreciation, or otherwise, of the show on offer. Most reviews punctuate their reports with interjections and actual responses from audience members including, for example '(applause)' and '(hear, hear)', 'cheer[ing] and hiss[ing] as the political feelings of the mixed audience prompted'.[3] One review notes that in the Assembly Hall, Wicklow, 'whistling, yelling, smoking and … interruptions is [sic] allowed a free hand'.[4]

In addition, the vast majority of entertainments of the period were structured along the lines of a meeting, a format which presupposed both visibility and participation. A chairperson was nominated to introduce and preside over the entertainment and, at the close of the proceedings, to make a few remarks and to propose a vote of thanks to the provider(s) of the evening's amusement. The motion was then seconded by a member of the audience, who often added their own remarks. The vote was then put to the audience and passed or rejected accordingly. The entertainer would also reply and the evening would be concluded with the singing of the national anthem, an appropriate hymn or, in the case of nationalist entertainments, an appropriate ballad. This structure, familiar to all, served to reinforce the social, communal and convivial aspects of the event while retaining the formal structure necessary to the smooth running of the show.

1 *Clonmel Chronicle*, 10 Feb. 1900, p. 2.   2 *Sligo Champion*, 23 May 1896, p. 5.   3 *Tuam Herald*, 13 Oct. 1900, p. 2.   4 *Wicklow Newsletter*, 22 Nov. 1902, p. 2.

REALISM

In considering the impact of the first cinematograph pictures on audiences, it has been common in the relevant literature to emphasize their 'uncanny' realism as a primary draw. The promoters of cinematographic entertainments in provincial Ireland foregrounded the 'scientific amusement'[5] provided by 'one of the greatest wonders of the age'.[6] The *Clonmel Chronicle* published this notice in 1897, alerting the public to the attractions of the cinematograph in advance of the town's first screening:

THE CINEMATOGRAPH. FIRST VISIT TO CLONMEL

> One of the most popular of what may be termed scientific amusements that have been given to the public is undoubtedly the Cinematograph or 'Animated Pictures'. It is absolutely the most attractive and entertaining of known inventions – in fact no invention yet brought out for the amusement and edification of the public can be compared with it and none have been received with greater surprise and acclamation. It is positively the greatest and most mystifying wonder of photography and electricity known, and its marvels are difficult to realise ... in every respect true to life, and with every movement as though the actual reality were before us.[7]

The promotional discourse of the notice makes several key assumptions about the prospective customers it hopes to attract. Firstly, it is assumed that the public are familiar with the name of Edison and his work. Making use of the familiar language of marvel that accompanied the name internationally, the notice reproduces a sense of excitement about advances in technologies of entertainment and replicates the rhetoric of wonder and awe common to the promotion of scientific novelties throughout the nineteenth century. The invocation of science, invention and edification as primary attractions also signal the respectability of the entertainment.

The language of the notice, however, signals a curious ambivalence to the realism of the representation. Described as 'mystifying' and 'difficult to realise' yet 'in every respect true to life ... as though the actual reality were before us,' it recalls Gunning's suggestion that nineteenth-century conceptions of cinematic realism owed more to the traditions of magic theatre and presentations of popular science, designed to astound and baffle rather than transparently to reveal reality.[8] This ambivalence surrounding the 'reality' of cinematograph images is

5 *Clonmel Chronicle*, 13 Feb. 1897, p. 3.   6 *Ballymoney Free Press*, 2 Dec. 1897, p. 2.   7 *Clonmel Chronicle*, 17 Feb. 1897, p. 2.   8 Tom Gunning, 'The cinema of attractions: early film, its spectator and the avant-garde' in T. Elsaesser (ed.), *Early Cinema: space, frame, narrative* (London,

also a feature of audience reactions in provincial Ireland. Thus, while photographic slides and cinematographic films appear to have been accepted as 'true' records of objects and events, there was also a degree of scepticism amongst audiences concerning the 'realism' of what was shown. On the one hand, a significant number of reviews discuss the 'vivid and lifelike' and 'singularly realistic' nature of cinematograph films.[9] The exhibition of cinematograph images of the visit of the newly crowned Edward VII to Belfast, for example, prompted a reviewer to comment that 'the scenes were brought so clearly before the audience that it was almost impossible to get rid of the idea that the onlookers were part of the vast assembly in Belfast on that historic occasion'.[10] On the other hand, the realism of the images was often challenged or ignored.

A broad range of reviews of cinematographic entertainments in the local press, for example, comment upon the perceived poverty of the images screened relative to the known, or speculated, reality. The *Ballymoney Free Press* in 1899 published this quite damning criticism of a cinematograph exhibition:

> By the aid of Lumière's cinematograph, the Oceanic was launched in Craigatimpin Hall on Friday evening last. The launch passed off without any loss of life or limb and, like many other things in life, there was more pleasure in the anticipation than in the realisation. The representation of the launch of the Oceanic does not possess anything very exciting; in fact, the launch may be described as flat.[11]

In stark contrast to prevalent rhetorics of shock and astonishment that purportedly accompanied the first cinema screenings, it appears that this particular reviewer didn't find the film either astonishing or realistic enough. There is also evidence of a degree of scepticism concerning the extent to which cinematograph pictures could be reliably considered as genuine records of the events they represented. The reviewer of the *Sligo Champion*, for example, describes cinematograph images as 'counterfeit presentments',[12] a description which is echoed in a reviewer's reports of Edison's Pictures in Tuam. Questioning the authenticity of some of the films, particularly one of President Kruger fleeing government buildings following defeat in the Boer War, the *Herald*'s reviewer reports that 'the thought came over us, as we looked, that ... [how] the camera man could have gotten hold of this dramatic scene, where he found space, and when, at the dramatic moment, he found the fleeing President to pose [was possible] ... It may be said that everything true was fancied and that everything that was fanciful and fascinating was not true'.[13]

1990), pp 56–62. 9 *Clonmel Chronicle*, 10 Feb. 1900, p. 2. 10 *Ballymoney Free Press*, 17 Dec. 1903, p. 4. 11 *Ballymoney Free Press*, 9 Feb. 1899, p. 2. 12 *Sligo Champion*, 22 Feb. 1902, p. 8. 13 *Tuam Herald*, 6 Sept. 1902, p. 2.

RECOGNITION AND LOCAL CONTENT

Despite this ambivalence concerning the realistic qualities of cinematograph images, a key pleasure of such entertainments for early Irish audiences was nonetheless that of recognition. The reviews published throughout my data sample clearly indicate a strong preference for local material. The *Drogheda Argus* reports that, during a visit of Edison's Animated Pictures to the town in 1902, '[c]onsiderable disappointment was evinced by the ... audience ... when they discovered that no local scenes were to be shown on the occasion'. It seems likely that this disappointment was made known to the exhibitor since on the following day, 'three local pictures were thrown upon the screen for the admiration of the audience'.[14] The same publication, reporting on the exhibition of the Animatograph at Kilsaran, observes that '[t]he special cinematograph pictures thrown on the screen were the great Bute wedding at Kilsaran on July 6th, 1905 ... Everyone present, in fact, saw the whole wedding right through again, and recognized themselves or their friends as if they were in reality'.[15] The *Sligo Champion*, for example, describes the delight of the audience at Edison's Animated Pictures 'who identified the exact "counterfeit presentment" of many old friends such as that worthy Soggarth Aroon, Canon Loftus of Ballymote, Alderman Connolly and that veteran John Ferguson. They walked in front of the audience as large as life and it is needless to say that they met with a kindly reception'.[16]

In his study of the reception of late Imperial Russian cinema, Yuri Tsivian found that familiar faces on the screen would evoke sinister motifs of doubles, duality and death.[17] By contrast, provincial Irish audiences appear to have been, first and foremost, amused by the depiction of themselves on screen, 'creat[ing] rounds of laughter as those in the audience recognized themselves or their neighbours in the living pictures ... ye gods! How we laughed'.[18] For Uli Jung, the key significance of local films is the mode of reception rather than production: the audience watching themselves, their locality and events on screen.[19] Similarly, the viewers of local material in my research appear to have been solicited on the basis of their local knowledge. While a stranger, watching local images and films, could produce no more than general meanings, the appeal of these images for locals involved a different kind of emotional engagement and public recognition.

Recalling the antipathy of the *Tuam Herald*'s reviewer to the 'counterfeit' nature of cinematographic representation, it is tempting to think of the

---

14 *Drogheda Argus*, 15 Feb. 1902, p. 4.   **15** *Drogheda Argus*, 18 Nov. 1905, p. 4.   **16** *Sligo Champion*, 22 Feb. 1902, p. 8.   **17** Yuri Tsivian, *Early Cinema in Russia and its cultural reception*, (Chicago, 1994).   **18** *Sligo Champion*, 17 Jan. 1903, p. 5.   **19** Uli Jung, 'Local Views: A blind spot in the historiography of early German cinema', *Historical Journal of Film, Radio and Television*, 22: 3 (2002), pp 253–73.

preference for local content as a guarantee of authenticity. Mobilizing local knowledge as confirmation of the image-as-genuine requires that the audience attend the exhibition and themselves evaluate the authenticity of images. The demand for local content thus provides a telling example of audiences' capacity to interpret the image according to cultural preference. The provincial Irish enthusiasm for local material, encouraging engagement and involvement rather than distanced and anonymous appreciation of a mass cultural spectacle, signals a preference for entertainment marked by participation rather than spectacular distance.

DOMINANCE OF ORAL CULTURE

A variety of theorists have remarked upon the absence of an established and robust visual culture in Ireland during the period in question.[20] Kevin Rockett, for example, claims that 'the word has dominated, and continues to overpower, the visual in Irish cultural life'.[21] If this is so, then it is possible to see how the visual aspects of cinematograph picture were downplayed and appropriated according to familiar perceptual templates. Thus, in provincial Ireland, the inevitable presence and activity of the lecturer in cinematograph exhibitions as a mediator of the images on screen was never regarded as compensatory or ancillary. Indeed, what often appeared to matter most to reviewers was not the visual impact of the images cast upon the screen but the quality and content of the accompanying oratory. As a result, it was not uncommon for entertainment reviews to ignore the exhibition of the cinematograph, other than to comment curtly on the operator's skill, and concentrate on detailed description and analysis of the quality of the lecture and its delivery.

A lecturer of recognized ability was frequently the primary attraction of an entertainment. 'Research, lucidity of style and vividness of narration'[22] were expected. 'Delicacy of touch and charm'[23] were appreciated, 'brilliant flashes of wit and humour'[24] admired, and fluency and the ability to speak 'entirely from memory'[25] preferred. Ineptitude and lack of eloquence were simply not tolerated. The *Sligo Champion* of 1897 offers this commentary on the inadequate performance of one such lecturer:

> From the commencement, Mr. M'Carthy gave evidence that lecturing was not his forte. He may be a very practical man, and we believe

20 Adele Dalsimer and Vera Kreilcamp (eds), *Visualising Ireland: national identity and the pictorial tradition* (London, 1993); Lelia Doolan, 'A debate on media and popular culture,' *The Crane Bag*, 8 (1984), pp 175–91.   21 Kevin Rockett, 'From Atlanta to Dublin,' *Sight and Sound* (June 1992), p. 26.   22 *Ballymoney Free Press*, 19 Oct. 1905, p. 2.   23 *Ballymoney Free Press*, 27 Feb. 1896, p. 2.   24 *Ballymoney Free Press*, 19 Oct. 1905, p. 2.   25 *Clonmel Chronicle*, 22 Apr. 1899 p. 2.

he is ... but as a lecturer, he is not in it. The matter of his lecture may have been excellent ... but he read the Manuscript in such a low tone of voice as to make his utterance unheard beyond a limited space in the front seats.[26]

A later report demonstrates a long memory on the part of Sligo audiences:

Owing to the former miserable failure on the part of a party who advertised himself as a lecturer ... the people [were] rather wary of trusting another ... But Mr. Lynd was the opposite to the first fraud, for he knew what he was speaking about and could impart his knowledge in a most attractive and receivable form ... Mr. Lynd possesses all the characteristics of a popular lecturer.'[27]

As this particular example suggests, the reputation, personality and performance of the lecturer were not only important in the entertainment of audiences but in determining how the images on screen were to be perceived as well.

Like those described by Braun and Keil, 'the most popular lecturers – the ones that found the greatest praise in the newspapers – were local; popular ... because of their familiarity with the audience as well as their subject'.[28] Trading on local knowledge of local events or personalities, lecturers were able to supply a context, and add extra layers of meaning, to the products of filmmakers from other nations. In this way, the quality of the lecturer and his address could materially affect the film's reception. However, while provincial Irish audiences clearly enjoyed the local element provided by lecturers, it would be a mistake to impose an overly rigid binarism between the 'oral' and the 'visual'. As noted above, the visual qualities of cinematograph films *were* recognized and appreciated. It therefore seems likely that the relative emphasis on the spoken word was also the product of the activities of the Catholic church and the Gaelic League.

THE CLERGY, THE GAELIC LEAGUE AND POPULAR CULTURE

Horace Plunkett, writing in 1904, described the enormous influence of the clergy in late nineteenth- and early twentieth-century provincial Ireland: 'In no other country in the world, probably, is religion so dominant an element in the daily life of the people and certainly, nowhere else has the minister of religion so wide and undisputed an authority'.[29] It is reasonable to suggest that a

26 *Sligo Champion*, 30 Jan. 1897, p. 5. **27** *Sligo Champion*, 9 Oct. 1897, p. 5. **28** Marta Braun and Charlie Keil, 'Sounding Canadian: early sound practices and nationalism in Toronto-based exhibition,' in R. Abel and R. Altman (eds), *The sounds of early cinema* (Bloomington, 2001), pp 198–204. **29** Horace Plunkett, *Ireland in the new century* (Dublin, 1982, orig. 1904), p. 94.

different notion of cinematograph reception can be inferred from exhibition practices in which the participation and sanction of the clergy in organizing, supervising or presenting exhibitions prevailed. In the Town Halls, churches, temperance halls and schoolrooms of provincial Ireland, the salience of the religious presence in approving, organizing and conducting cinematograph screenings was widespread during the period under review. The Church's right to grant or refuse access to venues under their control effectively functioned as a form of regulation of exhibitions and their content in the years before official censorship legislation was applied. In this context, the role of the clergy in disparaging and resisting 'indecent' forms of leisure in favour of cultivating pastimes of an 'improving' or 'instructive' nature became prevalent.

As Scott McQuire has remarked, 'cinema was the place in which an avowedly secular society prepared itself to encounter the other – the foreign, the fantastic, the erotic'.[30] The participation of the clergy in controlling the exhibition context suggests a strategy of regulation of the use of the cinematograph to prevent, or at least to curtail, the exercise of its secular potential, a strategy underpinned by the project of cultural nationalism. As Rockett has noted, the coordination of the efforts of national protectionist campaigns and the institutional Catholic church effected a suppression of such entertainments and that cinema, in this climate, was 'already a marked medium'.[31]

On 25 November 1892, Douglas Hyde presented his initial manifesto for cultural revival to the National Literary Society. From this beginning, *Conradh na Gaeidhlige* was formed, growing from forty-three branches in 1897 to two hundred and twenty-seven branches by 1902 and almost six hundred branches, with a membership approaching 50,000, by 1904. Hyde's initial manifesto for cultural revival, and the subsequent founding of the Gaelic League, in effect created a binary opposition: organic, native peasant culture versus constructed, alien British culture. Thus, from the very outset of the revival, popular culture *in general* tended to be depicted as an unwelcome, foreign force, corroding the purity of indigenous Irish cultural heritage.

As Gaelic League membership burgeoned, a palpable shift in the cultural climate began to occur. Once local Gaelic League branches became established and prospered, the rural, peasant, native entertainments, so highly praised by the League, became the most common and prominent items on concert bills. The public's response to those changes, as reflected in the published reviews, also changed. For not only did the Gaelic League's objectives begin to dictate the types of entertainment considered appropriate but shape the content of these entertainments as well. *Feiseanna, Aeriodheachta* and *Sgoruidheachta* become regular features in the provincial entertainment calen-

30 Scott McQuire, *Visions of modernity: representation, memory, time and space in the age of the camera* (London, 1998), p. 216. 31 Kevin Rockett, *Irish film censorship: a cultural journey from silent cinema to internet pornography* (Dublin, 2004), p. 19.

dar as a more culturally appropriate alternative to the 'polluting filth' and 'vulgarities' of the music hall. Lectures began to feature Irish subjects and themes 'to enlighten Irishmen on their own country'[32] and spread 'a knowledge of history and … pride in native civilisation and language'.[33] Concerts increasingly promoted songs 'in our grand old mother tongue,' and ballads such as 'Come Back to Erin,' 'Eileen Aroon' and 'The West's Asleep', along with recitations such as 'An Appeal for the Irish Language', selections of instrumental Irish airs, Irish dancing, whistling solos of Irish tunes and gramophone selections of Irish music and song.

The Gaelic League's antipathy to British popular culture, so explicitly criticized by Douglas Hyde, became a key concern for provincial entertainment seekers. The League's success in cultivating among its members a pride in native rural pastimes had resonance beyond Hyde's rhetoric. The League became, in many districts, synonymous with wholesome, quality entertainment. The previously popular concert items of comic songs and stage-Irishisms were also to receive the most vitriolic and unrelenting criticism as a 'vulgar English view of ourselves as uninformed, illiterate buffoons … a picture of obscenity and degradation … [and] an insult to public taste'.[34]

In this context, music hall, in particular, became the *bête noire* of the League. Inevitably, this had consequences for the reception of the cinematograph insofar as the variety format was the most common way for the Irish provincial public to witness cinematograph exhibitions at this time. Performances consisted of a series of short, unconnected films alternating with and sandwiched between a discontinuous and enticing range of comic and sentimental songs and recitations, short plays and skits, instrumental music and dances with which they competed and against which they were evaluated. While the cinematograph was not specifically castigated by Hyde or the League, its involvement in a vaudeville or variety format meant that it too, at least indirectly, suffered in terms of popularity under the revivalist programme.

Irish items were explicitly and actively encouraged in the preparation of concert programmes: The *Kerry Sentinel* of 2 November 1898 published this review of a variety concert held in Kenmare:

> The alarming extent to which the Anglicisation of our music and songs has reached is painfully evident from the perusal of reports in the Provincial press of popular entertainments. Take the remote town of Kenmare, Co. Kerry, for instance, situated in a district where sixty percent of the people are Irish-speaking. Here at least one would expect to find some lingering appreciation of our beautiful native music but alas! The detestable English music hall song holds sway … The

32 *Drogheda Argus*, 6 Feb. 1904, p. 4.   33 *Drogheda Argus*, 28 Jan. 1905, p. 4.   34 *Kerry Sentinel*, 3 Dec. 1903, p. 2.

havoc being wrought on the national character by this wholesale sup-
planting of our native songs by the product of the London music hall
is so serious as to merit the attention of every Irishman who seeks the
merit of his country. The fact that the popular song of Whitechapel
also finds applause in Kerry is positive proof that we are being assim-
ilated by the 'imperialist race' and are being degraded in the process.

By contrast, the *Tuam Herald* of 11 November 1898 carries this review of a
Feis Ceoil held in Galway:

One of the chief characteristics of this competition and concert [of
Irish music, song and dance] where the performers are all peasants,
was what might have been a surprise to most people, but none to me,
namely a complete absence of all vulgarity – that hideous art defiler
which stalks like a skeleton at most art feasts of the present day ...
while the inhabitants of shabby England are often vulgar, the Celtic
peasants of the uncontaminated West are naturally poetical and refined,
and that is the explanation of the fact that all vulgarity was absent
from this little music festival of peasants.

In the Irish context, it is reasonable to argue that the Gaelic League's broad
influence on Irish culture and leisure produced an antipathy towards *any* entertainment that could not be considered 'national,' 'local' and 'Gaelic'. Inevitably,
this reinforced a demand for local material, and customization of cinematographic presentations, as both a way of reinforcing the objectives of the organization as well as avoiding possible criticism.

The intervention of the Gaelic League, therefore, provides an example of
a situation in which both the exhibition and reception of visual media were
shaped and positioned by the larger forces of Irish history. Fearful of the
encroachment of imported entertainment and of a mass culture in the making,
the Gaelic League appointed itself to the role of cultural gatekeeper or autho-
rizing 'agent' and determined which cultural activities should be deemed
worthy or not. In this way, the Gaelic League's direct intervention in the
provincial leisure calendar, strongly supported by the Catholic church, became
a calculated and tactical response to the cultural encroachment of 'alien' mass
culture and secular entertainment in which the project of cultural revival
expressed itself in the form of cultural control.

CONCLUSION

The investigation of cinematograph spectatorship in a provincial Irish context
suggests that viewers drew on the familiar structures and practices of their

culture, with its focus on the voice, performance, immediacy and participation. The audience's sense of itself was of a social, collective gathering. The prevailing exhibition context was fundamentally different from that of later classical cinema, offering an experience in which audience visibility, mobility and participation were the norm. In this context, the reception of the cinematograph in provincial Ireland demonstrates the key characteristics of participation and communality.

The explicit preference of provincial Irish audiences was also for entertainment items that sustained and enhanced the collective, participatory relations between viewer and viewed. This preference for participatory engagement, whether in recognizing the faces and places on screen or in contributing comments and appreciation (or otherwise), was also supported by the clergy and cultural nationalists whose religious and political goals reinforced the local appropriation of 'foreign' matter and sustained the collectively regulated nature of the exhibition experience.

Partitionist viewing – the split in newsreel coverage of Ireland during the Second World War

CIARA CHAMBERS

'Fencing in Ireland'[1], 'baby boxers'[2] (covering an infant boxing match), and 'balloon houses' ('inexpensive igloos while you wait!')[3] were just some of the titles which appeared as part of specially edited cinema newsreels produced exclusively for southern Irish audiences during World War II. While trivial, quirky items like these were mainstays of the standard newsreel at the height of its popularity in the 1930s, the content of the newsreel changed considerably on the outbreak of war for audiences throughout Britain and Northern Ireland, but not for viewers in the south of Ireland. This split in viewing mirrored the widening gap between north and south, and indeed the growing manifestation of partition in the Irish public's psyche.

By the 1930s, newsreels were a standard feature of every cinema programme, first appearing in Britain in 1910 and providing the general public with the only form of on-screen news available until the advent of television in the 1950s. They were issued bi-weekly to match programme changes in the cinema and covered several news items in around ten minutes. Given that the public had access to more immediate news through radio and newspapers, the newsreels provided the visuals to items that were often already familiar to audiences. Apart from *Irish Events* (1917–20) there were no regular indigenous Irish newsreels until the *Amharc Éireann* series began in 1956. In the intervening years, Ireland was covered by and catered for by outside news producers, which inserted Irish items into their British release editions. Although newsreels approached politics with caution, they were nonetheless subject to constraints in both Britain and Ireland. In the south of Ireland, the Official Film Censor kept offscreen images of British royalty that might cause audience disturbance, while the IRA often took direct action against cinemas showing footage of royal weddings or coronations. Film censorship in Britain was more diffuse, split between the industry body, the British Board of Film Censors (established in 1912), and local authorities which retained powers under the Cinematograph Act, 1909. As a result of a loophole, newsreels

1 Pathé Gazette, *Fencing in Ireland*, 41/82 (13 Oct. 1941). 2 Gaumont British, *Baby Boxers*, 871 (11 May 1942). 3 Pathé Gazette, *Balloon Houses*, 41/97 (4 Dec. 1942).

escaped formal censorship in Britain but newsreel companies were keen not to jeopardise their privileged position by tackling controversial subjects. During the Second World War, the content of newsreels became of acute interest to both British and Irish governments. In Britain, news material was censored by the Ministry of Information at source while, in Ireland, a policy of neutrality was maintained. As a result, what audiences on different sides of the border were able to see differed significantly.

Whereas audiences in Northern Ireland, as throughout the UK, watched newsreels which contained an estimated eighty-five per cent of war news,[4] in Éire any mention of the war in the cinema was severely restricted under the government's strict policy of censorship. As a neutral state, operating under the Emergency Powers Act, any criticism of a belligerent, in effect any Allied film attacking the Germans, was forbidden. This included films containing war-front news, preparations for war, or propaganda against a belligerent. Kevin Rockett suggests that the policy of neutrality adopted by the Irish government meant 'in practice' that 'the Irish state embarked on what the Minister for the Co-ordination of Defensive Measures, Frank Aiken, described as a form of "limited warfare", which allowed the Irish government to steer a middle-course between conflicting strains within Irish society'.[5] In this respect, the policy was less concerned with avoiding offence to a belligerent than maintaining internal social cohesion. Entering the war on the side of the Allies would have demonstrated support for Britain and therefore an implicit recognition of partition that was anathema to many Irish people. From the Irish government's viewpoint, neutrality was the option that divided the Irish people least and there was also the threat of a German-backed IRA revolt to contend with should Éire enter the war.[6] In practice, Éire pursued a policy of 'friendly neutrality' towards Britain, and Donal O'Drisceoil suggests that Irish assistance to the Allies elevated its neutral status to that of a 'non-belligerent'.[7] One hundred thousand Irish men and women worked in British munitions factories and over sixty thousand enlisted in the war effort. A total of seven hundred and eighty decorations, including eight Victoria Crosses, were awarded to southerners for their courage during the war.[8] Other features of assistance to the Allies during the war included the repatriation of Allied airmen while German military personnel were interned, the exchange of weather reports, and permission, from 1941, for Allied aircraft to fly over areas of Co. Donegal. Southern firemen also provided valuable assistance during the Belfast blitz for which the Northern Ireland authorities were to find themselves largely unprepared. This increasing assistance to the Allies had no place, howev-

4 Mass Observation, *Content of Newsreels*, File Report 22 (28 Jan. 1940). 5 Kevin Rockett, *Irish film censorship* (Dublin, 2004), p. 334. 6 Donal O'Drisceoil, *Censorship in Ireland, 1939–1945* (Cork, 1996), p. 3. 7 Ibid., p. 7. 8 Brian Barton, *Northern Ireland in the Second World War* (Belfast, 1995), p. 111.

er, in the Irish government's public campaign, fuelled by strict censorship, as it sought to assert Ireland's 'illusion of strict impartiality'.[9] It was most important in this period of still emerging independence that Ireland was not seen to be consorting with the 'old enemy'.[10]

NEWSREELS AND THE WARTIME IMAGE OF IRELAND

On the outbreak of war, the Irish government passed the Emergency Powers Act which described Ireland's current neutral status as a state of 'Emergency'. The Censorship of Films Act was amended through an Emergency Powers Order extending the powers of the Official Film Censor to cover propaganda concerning *any* belligerent. News films were to be free from war news: images of war were only to be permitted if the protagonists could not be identified and the commentary was objective.[11] So while audiences in Northern Ireland watched the upbeat, rallying newsreels designed to improve morale and increase production, just across the border in the South, cinemagoers saw no evidence whatsoever of global conflict on their screens. Irish audiences were presented with 'a radically different world to that shown to their British counterparts, a world into which the tribulations of their near neighbours and the war in Europe did not impinge'.[12] In commenting on cuts to a Pathé newsreel covering German bombs dropped in Dublin in 1941, Kevin Rockett describes 'an almost hysterical fear of informing cinemagoers of the reality of war and its devastating impact in Ireland, as elsewhere'.[13]

British newsreels commonly shown in Irish cinemas were so heavily edited that there was very little footage left. Three companies, Pathé, Gaumont and Movietone, produced Irish editions, combining international items, particularly from America, on non-war matters with items of local interest. Movietone's Irish edition, *Irish Movietone News*, sourced some of its material from the Irish Army's film unit, which provided footage of defence force parades and military training exercises. While the pictures were shot by the army, contextualizing commentary was added by Movietone. Military parades throughout the country were regularly featured in *Irish Movietone News*, assuring Irish audiences that the country was well defended against any potential enemy in the midst of what was described as 'a time of gravest danger' in one item showing characteristic reluctance to use the word 'war'.[14] The subject of international conflict hovers over these displays of national unity but emphasis is concentrated on internal defensive measures rather than on outside events. Repeated scenes of huge neutrality rallies are described as 'gigantic'[15] in Drogheda; the

9 O'Drisceoil, *Censorship in Ireland*, p. 7.   10 Ibid.   11 Rockett, *Irish film censorship*, p. 338. 12 O'Drisceoil, *Censorship in Ireland*, p. 33.   13 Rockett, *Irish film censorship*, p. 339.   14 Irish Movietone News, *Colours for the LDF*, Story No. 42809A (1942).   15 Irish Movietone News,

'biggest military parade ever to be seen in the city'[16] in Cork; the 'largest known march in Wexford'[17]; 'huge crowds' packing the streets of Tralee;[18] and as 'impressive scenes in Dundalk'.[19] The use of superlatives in the commentary is matched by pictures of orderly uniformed volunteers watched by large crowds, presided over by the imposing figure of Taoiseach Eamon de Valera, attired completely in black, often in contrast to a sea of nurses in pristine white uniforms. In his speeches, the volunteers are frequently praised for their service to their country, and appeals are commonly made for more volunteers, and for supplies of clothing and money. A priest often blesses military colours and the troops are inspected by de Valera or another government representative. The Taoiseach frequently walks briskly through lines of military personnel, seemingly oblivious to the troops he is inspecting. In one item he rushes along a line of troops so quickly he almost stumbles.[20] Conversely, when the vast lines of military personnel march past de Valera, we can often see their faces turn upwards to gaze at the Taoiseach, who is usually positioned on a raised platform as a symbol of unfaltering Irish self-determination.

Military training exercises also appear in the *Irish Movietone News* series. Such training includes, as the British-inspired commentary puts it, 'mock' or 'imaginative bombing attacks',[21] Army medical training where 'occasionally there's a genuine casualty, by accident perhaps',[22] and scenes of marine service exercises proving it is 'in a constant state of readiness to defend Ireland's shores'.[23] Often the volunteers training are shown having tea or meals after their work, since, we are told, 'Irishmen are notoriously fond of their cup of tea'.[24] These scenes serve to highlight the fact that these are merely training exercises, and Ireland is not suffering the reality of war. One item shows the Construction Corps enjoying their outdoor work in the sunshine. At lunchtime they eat what is shown in close-up to be a hearty meal, even though the commentary tells us 'today's Friday, a fast day, but it looks pretty good for a fast day'.[25] After lunch the men, on their half day off, are shown playing baseball and swimming. In another item, dealing with 'holiday training' for the Citizen Army, the commentary states 'and now to the more serious business of get-

---

LDF Recruiting Parade at Drogheda, BFI, Ref No. 45205A (1942).   **16** Irish Movietone News, *Army Parade – Dublin, Cork*, Story No. 42891 (30 Sept. 1942).   **17** Gaumont British News, *Big Parade at Wexford*, Issue 816 (30 Oct. 1941).   **18** Irish Movietone News, *De Valera at Tralee*, Story No. 41560 (11 Oct. 1941).   **19** Irish Movietone News, *LDF Parade*, Story No. 42965 (16 Oct. 1942).   **20** Gaumont British News, *Mr de Valera at Mullingar*, Issue 813 (20 Oct. 1941). Many of Gaumont's Dublin issues used the same footage as *Irish Movietone News* – the pooling of footage between newsreel companies was common practice during wartime.   **21** Irish Movietone News, *De Valera Reviews ARP Parade*, Story No. 39847 (10 March 1940).   **22** Irish Movietone News, *Army Medical School – Ireland*, Story No. 41731 (22 Dec. 1941).   **23** Irish Movietone News, *Marine Service*, Story No. 42756 (24 Aug. 1942).   **24** Irish Movietone News, *An Army Marches on Its ...* Story No. 41596 (20 Nov. 1941).   **25** Irish Movietone News, *Construction Corps at Work in Éire's Forests*, BFI , Ref No. 204581A (1941).

ting rifles. What's the use of a soldier without a gun?' At this point shots of
a soldier handing out guns from the back of a truck are juxtaposed with a
scene of seated soldiers peeling potatoes while the commentary describes 'activity of another kind', namely 'a course in potato peeling'. 'Wait', the commentator gushes, 'till their wives and mothers see these'. Immediately attention
is drawn away from the rifle, the masculine weapon of war, to the preparation of food which the commentary identifies as a feminine pastime. The juxtaposition of rifle with food appears in another item covering Local Defence
Force training which cuts quickly from scenes of snipers taking part in an
exercise to a shot of an ice-cream seller offering 'Kavanagh's Pure Ices' to the
soldiers who are smiling and, as the commentary states, 'fraternizing round
the ice cream barrel'. The item's concluding remark sums up the British view
of the work of the Irish military – 'it's a grand life'.[26]

The disparaging tone of these British newsreels is hard to ignore, but they
never overtly suggest that Irish defences are less than adequate. Indeed, some
of these scenes would have appeared in British newsreels to illustrate to the
British public that Ireland could resist attack against Germany, and indeed
Britain, if necessary. Most of the footage provided by the army would, however, have been viewed only by audiences in the south of Ireland. Of twenty-
three reels of *Irish Movietone News* held by the British Film Institute dating
between 1940–3 (comprising one-hundred-and-twenty items), a third of the
material deals with topics of a military nature. The rest includes local sport-
ing events, religious parades, society weddings and general trivia. In general,
these 'neutralized' newsreels allowed the cinemagoing public to view news
similar in shape and content to that of the pre-war era. However, Kevin
Rockett writes of the relief felt by cinema exhibitors when these newsreels
ceased in 1943 due to a shortage of film stock in Britain. The Irish public, it
seemed, had long tired of the often inane nature of cinema newsreels which
told nothing about the war but regularly featured Dublin's Zoo or other
innocuous items.[27] The experience of audiences in Northern Ireland and Britain
was very different.

In the early stages of war, newsreels for British audiences and those in
Northern Ireland were not hostile in their portrayal of Éire's neutrality, but,
as the Treaty ports handed back by Britain in 1938 became of increasing strate-
gic importance, the tone began to change. Initially the main concern of British
newsreel companies was to convince the public in both Britain and Northern
Ireland that Ireland was ready to defend herself against the threat of German
invasion. As usual, skilful manipulation of image and commentary served the
newsreels' propagandistic purposes. When covering a pro-neutrality rally in
Dublin in 1940, Pathé's commentary suggested that its panning shots of vast

26 Irish Movietone News, *Éire's Cavalry on Wheels*, Story No. 41266 (9 May 1941).   27 Rockett,
Irish film censorship, p. 341.

crowds depicted a large rally supporting defensive measures against Germany. The commentary disingenuously tells the audience that 'Britain and Éire may not always have seen eye to eye in the past, but today all that is forgotten in the common danger'.[28] The newsreel attributes the three main political leaders with pro-defensive sentiments, sharing a platform to address huge crowds and stand united 'as a symbol of Éire's unity as she faces the danger of aggression'. The commentary suggests complete political support for the bolstering of Irish defences, thus fulfilling the newsreels' main objective at the time – to convince the British public that Éire was more than eager to defend herself against Germany and was expressing friendly and supportive sentiments towards Britain. A *Times* newspaper article offered a broader picture of the events depicted in the newsreel. Opposition leader William T. Cosgrave is reported to have stated that 'let none of the people be so foolish, so misguided as to give countenance and encouragement to any belligerent to invade the country,' while de Valera encouraged the Irish people to stand united behind the government 'ready to meet aggression from whatever quarter it may come'.[29] This demonstrates how newsreel commentary framed and manipulated images. The main emphasis of this rally was not, as the newsreel suggests, on defensive measures and a close wartime relationship with Britain but actually involved a declaration of Ireland's broad-based political support for neutrality and preparation for defence against an attack from *any* of the belligerents, including Britain.[30]

As the war progressed, irritation with the Irish government's uncompromizing neutral stance began to percolate into newsreel commentaries. After initially stressing the strength of Ireland's defences, a change in tone may be identified in the coverage of the bombing of Dublin in 1941, with one Pathé item concluding that 'maybe this is the price Éire has to pay for "sitting on the fence"'.[31] The most controversial newsreel of the period, *Ireland – the Plain Issue*, was produced by British Paramount News in February 1942. Robert Fisk suggests that the film 'sounded – and looked – as if it was intended to prepare the British public for an Allied invasion of Éire'.[32] In the ten-minute reel, dealing only with the subject of Irish neutrality, the Irish people are represented as backward, a pre-modern people associated with the land, and depicted as inherently different from the English. The film accuses de Valera of being a 'dictator', and leading a Catholic state which dislikes 'Protestant England.' Everything about this film is in direct opposition to the loyal Ulstermen said to be 'one hundred per cent' behind the war effort. The fiscal prowess and unbending loyalty of Ulstermen, 'wealthier than the Southern

28 Pathé Gazette, *All for Defence* Issue 40/50 (20 June 1940).   29 'Party Unity in Éire', *The Times* (29 May 1940).   30 Robert Fisk, *In time of war: Ireland, Ulster and the price of neutrality, 1939–45* (London, 1978), p. 336.   31 Pathé Gazette, *Germans Bomb Dublin* Issue 41/46 (9 June 1941).   32 Fisk, *In time of war*, p. 338.

Irish, more enterprising, better businessmen', brings Northern citizens closer to English ideals of industry and progress, with Ulster depicted as an industrially powerful asset to the Allied war machine, while Éire languishes in a state of insular apathy.[33]

Although Northern Ireland's contribution to the war effort was certainly significant it was consistently lower than any other region in the UK.[34] There were claims from the Ministry of Aircraft Production that Short and Harland were working at sixty-five per cent efficiency and levels of morale were low and absenteeism high. Even though strikes were illegal in Northern Ireland from 1940, there were two-hundred-and-seventy throughout the war, suggesting that the sentiments expressed by Craigavon 'we are the king's Men and we shall be with you to the end'[35] were not passionately adhered to in all quarters, and certainly not to the extent suggested in *Ireland – the Plain Issue*, which firmly stated that no Ulsterman desired neutrality. Equally, Tom Harrisson, co-founder of Mass Observation, the social survey organization, observed that the wartime atmosphere in Northern Ireland was profoundly different to the rest of Britain. He commented on the overall 'slackness of the atmosphere' and the 'irritation and resentment' caused by the war.[36] Indeed, the Northern Ireland government minister John McDermott acknowledged that Northern Ireland was 'only half in the war'.[37]

Ireland – the Plain Issue was an unusual case – such a controversial attack was not standard newsreel style. Initially Paramount defended the film, telling the press that they 'attempted to present the full facts of the case' and did not believe that they had given 'ground for offence … to Catholics in Ireland or elsewhere'.[38] Kevin Rockett suggests that *The Plain Issue* 'does not seem to have been submitted to the Irish Film Censor because of its openly anti-Irish bias'[39] and so it would not have been shown in the south. It is possible that it may have been exhibited in some first-run cinemas in the north. Certainly, screenings of the newsreel in Britain lead to a complaint by John Dulanty, High Commissioner for Éire. It was subsequently withdrawn with apologies from Paramount and the excuse that the company's chairman and managing director had been in the US at the time of its release. Those responsible for the film, Paramount claimed, had been censured.[40]

Neutrality was dealt with in less forceful terms by a 1944 edition of the American newsreel March of Time entitled *The Irish Question*. March of Time usually ran for about twenty minutes, was concerned with one topic, and often used actors in staged scenes. The film begins with such a staged scene with

33 British Paramount News, *Ireland – the Plain Issue*, Issue 1140 (2 Feb. 1942).   34 Jonathan Bardon, *A history of Ulster* (Belfast, 1992), p. 580.   35 Bardon, *History of Ulster*, p. 581.   36 Barton, *Northern Ireland*, p. 16.   37 PRONI, CAB 4/473, 15 May 1941 in Barton, *Northern Ireland*, p. 24.   38 'Éire Objects to Film', *Daily Telegraph* (7 Feb. 1942), p. 3.   39 Rockett, *Irish film censorship*, p. 455n.   40 O'Drisceoil, *Censorship in Ireland*, p. 43.

the reading of George Bernard Shaw's wife's will. Referring to 'them – the Irish', she describes the Irish people as having 'awkward manners … vulgarities of speech and other defects'. She leaves money to 'teach the Irish self control, elocution, deportment, the art of personal contact and social intercourse'. The film goes on to explain life in the 'lovely and sorrowful land of St Patrick', handing over to an Irish commentator to do so. The language used by the commentator is musical and poetic and in stark opposition to the framework set up by the official March of Time commentary. Even so, we are reminded that few would swap places with an Irish farmer. Life is depicted as rural and strangely fascinating, a life to be marvelled at by the newsreel voyeur from the comfortable distance of the urban cinema. Freedom, we are told, 'has not brought riches to Ireland. We have lived too long and too intimately with poverty to be rid of it in a few short years'. But, the narrator explains, 'if this land is poor, it is still ours to make or marr'. Perhaps this sums up one of the most crucial aspects of the Irish decision to remain neutral: the Irish were seen to be stubborn followers of independence, despite the possible economic and social consequences. To opt out of a world war rather than compromise independence was somehow typically Irish. The juxtaposition with this suggestion with the exploration of Irish Catholicism can hardly be seen as coincidental. Religious faith in Ireland, it is stated, 'is no mere conviction, for deep in the Celtic nature is a hunger for the things of the spirit'; vocations to the priesthood bring honour upon Irish families, as 'there is no higher calling among the young men of Ireland'. Men of God help 'to form the character of the Irish people, their faith, their culture and their way of life'. In searching for an explanation of the Irish decision to remain neutral in a global war and thus to remain separate and marginalized, the film ultimately asks the viewer to 'look not to logic, but to the poetry of the Irish'.[41]

The Irish government expressed concern prior to the film's production about its depiction of neutral Éire, and Major Guilfoyle of military intelligence (G2) accompanied the film crew during production. Only one major issue was raised. Notes on the shooting script relating to shots of champagne being served at a dance in the Gresham hotel in Dublin called for the deletion of the scene due to the authorities' fear that it may have given 'a derogatory inflexion on their attitude on neutrality in a world at war'.[42] The scene was not included in the finished film and no further objections to *The Irish Question* were made. As Donal O'Drisceoil points out, in contrast to official priorities, no concern was expressed about scenes of barefoot children entering schools or the 'stereotypically patronising approach to the commentary'.[43] Concerns about the final film were, however, raised in advance by the film's

41 March of Time, *The Irish Question*, Issue 11–9th Year (12 June 1944).   42 Military Archives, Dublin, *'Film – March of Time'*, G2/X/1504, dope sheet for Roll 96 (undated).   43 O'Drisceoil, *Censorship in Ireland*, pp 44–5.

director, experimental British filmmaker Len Lye, who was employed by March of Time on a freelance basis to work on the film. In a report to G2, Major Guilfoyle suggested that Lye was

> not enamoured with March of Time methods in film commentary ... Lye reminded me on more than one occasion that he could take no responsibility for the eventual sub-editing and commentary. All he could do was to cover such aspects of the normal life of the country as would be of interest to the general body of cinemagoers in America. The subsequent editing and commentary by over emphasis, under-statement or deletion could give any film an undesirable slant.[44]

Despite the concerns expressed, the film was exhibited in both the north and south of Ireland, and indeed throughout the world.

It was only at the end of the war that films and newsreels banned by the Official Irish Censor appeared in cinemas. It was the first time in six years that war footage was readily available to Southern Irish audiences. Even then, however, newsreels covering the conflict remained contentious. Kevin Rockett gives the example of the Pathé item submitted in June 1945, just after the Emergency Powers Order was lifted, covering the bombing of Dublin's North Strand in 1941 referred to above, which was removed due to the 'sarcastic' remarks which 'would undoubtedly have caused offence'.[45] Indeed, when the war films began to flood into Irish cinemas in mid-1945, the worst fears of the authorities were realized as audiences divided along pro- and anti-British lines, cheering or jeering Allied successes. It was confirmation for the Irish authorities that its decision to keep off Irish screens any material relating to the war was justified as a means of maintaining public order in cinemas.

CONCLUSION

Philip Taylor suggests that 'censorship and propaganda are really different sides of the same medal: the manipulation of opinion'.[46] In this light, the British and Irish governments were both concerned with policing audience response to images of war. British newsreels encouraged audiences in the north to engage fully in the war effort and increase the value of industrial production. In the south, the government felt that it had to protect the country from harmful British propaganda but was also concerned, in the absence of an Irish news-reel, that the content of British and American newsreels would be anti-Irish.

---

44 Military Archives, Dublin, '*Film – March of Time*', G2/X/1504 Letter from Major Guilfoyle to C.S.O. G2 Branch 10 Dec. 1943.   45 Rockett, *Irish film censorship*, p. 339.   46 Philip M. Taylor, *British propaganda in the twentieth century* (Edinburgh, 1999), p. 153.

By purging newsreels of war news, audiences were reminded that, while they must rally to the defence of their country in a time of 'Emergency', World War II should not feature in their daily lives or places of entertainment. As a result, what we find in terms of newsreel coverage of World War II is not just varying representations of north and south but also a reflection of the solidification of partition, manifest in the differences in the news and propaganda offered to northern and southern audiences. The prevalence of war news for one audience, and the lack of it for another, reinforced a sense of division between the two parts of the country that reached its height near the end of the war. As the split in viewing meant that northern audiences had access to images of German concentration camps before those in the south, neutral Ireland's expression of condolences, through its Taoiseach, on the death of Adolf Hitler in May 1945 was seen as a repugnant act by people in both Britain and the North. According to Jonathan Bardon, de Valera's act led to a 'wave of disgust' amongst Northern Unionists that 'served as a reminder of how far the war had widened the gulf between north and south'.[47] Thus, just as broadcasting in the 1920s and 1930s contributed to the construction of what Martin McLoone describes as a 'partitionist mentality',[48] so the split in wartime newsreel viewing reinforced a growing sense of separation of the South of Ireland not only from the North but also the international community more generally.

47 Bardon, *History of Ulster*, p. 583.   48 Martin McLoone, 'The construction of a partitionist mentality: early broadcasting in Ireland' in McLoone (ed.), *Broadcasting in a divided community* (Belfast, 1996), pp 20–34.

'The States is brilliant': generic hybridity in *I Went Down* (1997) and *Divorcing Jack* (1998)[1]

KEVIN CUNNANE

Ireland's relationship with cinema is and has been intricately linked with the global. The first moving images of the country were recorded by representatives of Lumiére Brothers in 1896, while Ireland's first fiction film *The Lad From Old Ireland* (1910), was made by the American Kalem Company and directed by the Irish-Canadian Sidney Olcott. As Rockett, Gibbons and Hill indicate, American and British films continued to remain virtually the sole source of Irish film images until the mid-1970s.[2] Further links with international filmmaking industries were maintained through Irish émigrés working in Britain and Hollywood and the influence of what Rockett terms the 'cinema of the diaspora', Irish-themed films from countries with large Irish migrant communities.[3] Even when indigenous Irish filmmaking attracted international attention in the early 1990s with *My Left Foot* (Jim Sheridan, 1989), *The Crying Game* (Neil Jordan, 1992) and *In the Name of the Father* (Jim Sheridan, 1993), the films concerned had been financed primarily from British and American sources and had gained approval from the dominant film community in Hollywood through Oscar recognition. It is this influence of cinemas of other cultures, particularly Hollywood genre filmmaking, on indigenous Irish cinema that informs this essay. In this chapter I propose to examine the extent to which mainly Hollywood filmic practices have shaped and influenced two film texts: *I Went Down* (1997) and *Divorcing Jack* (1998). I argue that both films embrace a Hollywood-literate 'generic hybridity' but ultimately come unstuck due to the problems involved in transforming 'Ireland' into a fully convincing cinematic landscape.

Since the end of the First World War the United States had become and since maintained its dominance as the world's largest exporter of filmic audiovisual material.[4] This domination was especially prevalent in Ireland and, by the

1 Research for this essay was made possible by funding from the Higher Education Authority's North South Programme of Collaborative Research.   2 Kevin Rockett, Luke Gibbons and John Hill, *Cinema and Ireland* (London, 1988), p. xi.   3 Kevin Rockett, *The Irish filmography* (Dublin, 1996), p. 3.   4 See Kristin Thompson, *Exporting entertainment: America in the world film market, 1907–34* (London, 1985) and Ian Jarvie, *Hollywood's overseas campaign: The North Atlantic movie*

early 1930s, Irish cinemas were screening a higher proportion of American films than any other film-producing nation. The principal reasons for this were the lack of a competing indigenous industry, the shared use of the English language, the legacy of Irish emigration which cast the United States as modern and advanced, and the escape Hollywood cinema offered to a society dominated by an ethos of insular Catholic nationalism. As Rockett suggests, Hollywood films exhibited in Ireland provided 'an attractive and perhaps liberating alternative to official ideologies'.[5] The popularity of American films with Irish audiences continued despite the slow but gathering momentum of local film production throughout the 1970s and 1980s. Figures show that between 1980 and 1991 the market share of American films shown in Ireland never dropped below eighty-two per cent (see table below). With such a level of cultural saturation, it is not surprising that Irish filmmakers began to exhibit a degree of self-awareness towards American genre filmmaking. Similar to the audiences in the first half of the twentieth century, young Irish film practitioners are, according to Ruth Barton, deliberately adopting 'global filmmaking practices as a liberating strategy'.[6]

Table 1: US Share of Irish market (1980–1991) (%)

1980	1981	1982	1983	1984	1985	1986	1987	1988	1989	1990	1991
88	87	86	84	83	83	85	86	82	85	87	91.5

Source*: Screen Digest* and *European Audiovisual Observatory Statistical Yearbook 1994/5.*

HYBRIDITY AND FILM

According to Mikhail Bakhtin, hybridity may be defined as the 'mixture of two social languages within the limits of a single utterance'.[7] This concept has been subsequently utilized in the areas of colonialism, cultural theory and cinema. Thus, in the case of cinema, distinct genres and styles may be seen to merge into a new form, constituting what Robert Young describes as 'difference into sameness, and sameness into difference, but in a way that makes the same no longer the same, (and) the different no longer simply different'.[8] With reference to Hollywood cinema, Bordwell and Thompson also indicate how genre 'hybrids' have emerged as the result of 'cross-breeding'.[9] Although mixed-genre

trade, 1920–1950 (Cambridge, 1992).   **5** Kevin Rockett, 'Aspects of the Los-Angelesation of Ireland', *Irish Communications Review*, 1 (1991), p. 20.   **6** Ruth Barton, *Irish national cinema* (London, 2004), p. 123.   **7** Bakhtin cited in Robert Young, *Colonial Desire: hybridity in theory, culture and race* (London, 1995), p. 20.   **8** Young, *Colonial desire*, p. 26.   **9** David Bordwell and

films were common during the studio-driven, classic Hollywood period, Steve Neale argues that Hollywood cinema of the 1980s and 1990s placed a particular emphasis upon generic hybridity, the mixing and re-imaging of popular culture, and a taste for 'allusion and pastiche'.[10] Jim Collins also suggests how contemporary Hollywood film has been characterized by two related but opposing trends, identifiable by their adoption or rejection of hybridity. 'Eclectic irony' involves the dissonant, incongruous hybridization and juxtaposition of elements that don't belong together, while genre films of the 'new sincerity' reject ironic inter-generic melanges in favour of a single genre that recalls classic generic practices and 'a lost purity'.[11] As we shall see, it is this 'eclectic irony' that is also a feature of both *I Went Down* and *Divorcing Jack* although a degree of 'new sincerity' is evident in Breathnach's film.

HYBRIDITY IN IRISH CINEMA

The emergence of what can be described as 'Irish hybrid cinema' is evident as far back as the beginning of an indigenous cinema in the mid-1970s. Attempting to challenge the ownership of Irish cinematic imagery, the Irish 'New Wave' began merging Irish narratives with an aesthetic style more in common with European art cinema and the avant-garde. Pat Murphy's *Maeve* (1981) and Cathal Black's *Pigs* (1984), amongst others, are examples of this 'Euro-Irish' hybridization. However, one of the proponents of this school, Joe Comerford, whilst never a commercial filmmaker, also showed a willingness to integrate elements of Hollywood genre and European art cinema into his own distinct narratives.

In *Traveller* (1981) and *Reefer and the Model* (1988), elements of the American 'road movie' and 'chase movie' are juxtaposed with a European character-driven style more in common with other Irish New Wave films. McLoone reads Comerford's use of genre as pastiche, comically playing with the conventions of car chases and gun fights amidst a west of Ireland setting.[12] A more serious re-imagining of genre within an Irish context is found in *The Courier* (Joe Lee/Frank Deasy, 1987), the first indigenous Irish film to work openly within the gangster/thriller genre. As in *Taffin* (Francis Megahy, 1987), however, the mix of crime conventions and social issues proves only partly successful. *Eat the Peach* (1986) was one of the first indigenous Irish films to

Kristin Thompson, *Film art: an introduction*, 3rd edition (New York, 1990), p. 69. 10 Steve Neale, *Genre and Hollywood* (London, 2000), pp 248–9. 11 Jim Collins, 'Genericity in the Nineties: eclectic irony and the new sincerity', in Jim Collins, Hilary Radnery and Ava Preacher Collins (eds), *Film Theory Goes to the Movies* (New York), pp 242–63. 12 Martin McLoone, 'National cinema and cultural identity: Ireland and Europe', in John Hill, Martin McLoone and Paul Hainsworth (eds), *Border crossing: film in Ireland, Britain and Europe*, (Belfast and London, 1994), p. 163. See also Rockett, Gibbons and Hill, *Cinema and Ireland*, p. 273.

address the influence of American culture in Ireland. Peter Ormond's film specifically uses Hollywood cinema, in this case the Elvis Presley vehicle *Roustabout* (1964), as inspiration for two friends to devise a plan to reverse their financial and personal fortunes by building a motor-cycle 'wall-of-death' in the turf bogs of midlands Ireland. The use of comic books and jazz in *The Butcher Boy* (Neil Jordan, 1997), science fiction in *The Boy from Mercury* (Martin Duffy, 1996) and rock and roll in *Last of the High Kings* (David Keating, 1996) also indicate the concerns of later Irish films with the role of American popular culture in contemporary Ireland.

'I WENT DOWN'

The line, 'The States is brilliant', delivered in a thick Dublin accent by Bunny Kelly in a nondescript bar/nightclub in Gort, demonstrates the far-reaching influence of American culture on Irish cinema. The film playfully deconstructs this idealized notion of the United States in Irish consciousness when Bunny admits he has not actually been to America apart from 'on the telly and that'.[13] Bunny's perception of America is mediated through visual media and outwardly reflected in his appearance (Elvis-like sideburns and later his acquisition of leather cowboy boots) as well as his choice of literature (paperback Westerns). The Irish filmmakers (writer Conor McPherson, director Paddy Breathnach and producer Robert Warpole) are similarly immersed in American popular culture and their film, *I Went Down*, draws heavily on the conventions of Hollywood genre filmmaking.

Based on an original screenplay by playwright McPherson, *I Went Down* begins with Git (Peter McDonald), a young Dubliner who, not long after his release from prison, becomes beholden to gangster Tom French (Tony Doyle). In order to 'make things right', Git is paired with older criminal Bunny Kelly (Brendan Gleeson) to travel to Cork and collect a man, Frank Grogan (Peter Caffrey) who owes French £25,000. Their journey takes the pair through the back roads, forests and bogs of the midlands to Cork and back again but finding and holding onto Grogan proves more problematic.[14] From the plot description, it is already clear that two separate but not unconnected genres exist within *I Went Down* – the gangster film and the road movie. Visually, the influence of *film noir* is evident in the dimly-lit bars and pool halls and in the moody portraits of landscapes and forests. The coming together of two (subsequently three) mismatched protagonists also draws on the conventions

13 Conor McPherson et al., *I Went Down: the shooting script* (London, 1997), p. 67.   14 For accounts of the film's production see Paddy Breathnach and Robert Warpole, 'Two went down', *Film Ireland* (Oct./Nov. 1997), pp 12–13; Paul Power, 'The fine art of surfacing', *Film West*, (Oct. 1997), pp 16–19; and Gerald C. Wood, *Conor McPherson: imagining mischief* (Dublin, 2003).

of the buddy movie. Warpole describes the film as 'poly-generic' and Breathnach admits that they consciously 'wanted to make a genre film and play with genre'.[15] In effect, they have crafted a gangster/road movie comedy with debts to both film noir and the buddy movie.

According to Lance Pettitt, the film is 'unconcerned with socially-driven naturalism' and 'takes reference from other cinematic representations and is true to this medium rather than reality'.[16] Both Breathnach and McPherson have stated that they were unconcerned with fashioning a film preoccupied with 'Irishness' or re-examining the state of Irish identity.[17] An Irish setting and landscape provide the cultural context but generic hybridity and 'eclectic irony' take precedence. The gangster genre dominates with the character of Tom French having more in common with Italian-American screen gangsters than a representation of a real Dublin criminal such as Martin Cahill.[18] Breathnach's film owes more to contemporary reinterpretations of the gangster film à la Martin Scorsese (*Goodfellas*, 1990) or the Coen Brothers (*Miller's Crossing*, 1990) than the original 1930s genre itself. Given the film's self-awareness, the characters may be seen both to embrace and knowingly question the conventions of the gangster genre. Git questions Bunny's irrational need to steal while eagerly referring to the gun as a 'six-shooter'. While Bunny enthusiastically shows Git how to use a gun effectively, he also becomes annoyed by Git's constant use of the moniker, 'The Friendly Face'.

Barton considers *I Went Down* as belonging to a 'post-Tarantino Hollywood gangster cycle'.[19] Certainly, *I Went Down*'s opening title sequence and soundtrack bear similarities to the loud graphics and Californian guitars of *Pulp Fiction* (1994). However, while a number of late 1990s gangster films attempted to tap into the zeitgeist created by Tarantino, *I Went Down*'s combination of comedy and violence is nonetheless distinctive. Breathnach states:

> Maybe in an American landscape – Tarantino can sometimes do it – something cruel can be funny. But I feel in this landscape I just wouldn't have been able to do that.[20]

Reservoir Dogs and *Pulp Fiction* (1994) achieved a level of black comedy through their depiction of violent acts. In *I Went Down*, the representation of violence is either omitted or depicted within the conventions of a straight thriller. Git's

15 Power, 'The fine art of surfacing', p. 17. 16 Lance Pettitt, *Screening Ireland: film and television representation* (Manchester, 2000), p. 276. 17 McPherson admits that they didn't want to make a film that was 'specifically Irish' in Wood, *Conor McPherson* p. 150. Breathnach indicates that he deliberately wanted to 'move away from a lot of the clichés of Irish film' in McPherson et al., *I Went Down*, p. 113. 18 Cahill was the subject of three films, *The General* (John Boorman, 1998), *Ordinary Decent Criminal* (Thaddeus O'Sullivan, 1999) and *Vicious Circle* (David Blair, 1999). 19 Barton, *Irish national cinema*, p. 184. 20 McPherson et al., *I Went Down*, p. 115.

bar fight with French's thugs, the catalyst for his debt, happens off-screen with the audience learning later that one of the men lost an eye. The shootings of Grogan and French are revealed without any comic irony.

Hybridity in *I Went Down* is not solely confined to the influence of American genre filmmaking. Martin McLoone locates it within a new film culture employing both American and European influences.[21] Breathnach's debut feature *Alisa* (1994) is indebted to a European art film aesthetic synonymous with long takes and the privileging of characterization over plot and action. In *I Went Down*, Lance Pettitt points out that 'as a genre movie, character and scene take precedence over plot'[22] while McLoone describes it as 'poised between action and character'.[23] The road movie element of the narrative allows the characters to engage with one another whilst on the road or in the faceless pubs and hotels. Long passage of dialogue can be attributed to McPherson's theatrical background. His plays *Rum and Vodka* and *The Good Thief*, for example, are both one-character monologues exploring issues of masculinity and criminality.

The Irish landscape is not one that is immediately imaginable as the setting for expansive Hollywood genres such as the gangster film or road movie as *The Courier* proved in its problematic recasting of Dublin as the nameless gangster milieu.[24] Wisely in *I Went Down*, the narrative is expanded beyond Dublin and new environs are found by setting the action in the hinterland between the capital and Cork. Breathnach confirms the desire to 'explore an Irish world that maybe hadn't been seen before or maybe one that was very familiar in many respects but where we put a different spin on that landscape'.[25] The most effective of these are the bogs of the midlands described by Pettitt as 'identifiably Irish yet also shot to look like a US prairie'.[26] The Bog of Allen is romantically shot to evoke a metaphorical sense of space similar to the wide-open plains of the Arizona desert. Further links to the American Western are achieved through an unsettling solo harmonica score and a post-modern reference to the genre as Bunny flicks through his Western novel as Git takes Grogan through the bog to meet the 'Friendly Face'. A final homage is paid as Bunny and Git leave the bog, appearing to 'ride (drive) off into the sunset'.

Some commentators praised the film's representation of Dublin and Cork as clearly distinguishable urban locations with an accent, appearance, urban culture and a criminal style uniquely its own.[27] While the accents are clearly

21 McLoone, *Irish film*, pp 198–200.   22 Pettit, *Screening Ireland*, p. 275.   23 McLoone, *Irish film*, p. 199.   24 Ireland's lack of scale is jokily referred to by Breathnach: 'You can't really get lost in Ireland because you're only going to be twelve miles from any town' (Ciara Dwyer, 'A man who follows his own path', *Sunday Independent* (10 Oct. 2004), p. 5). McPherson states: 'It's a bit silly having a road movie in Ireland because you arrive very quickly' (James Christopher, 'The problem with Irish road movies is that you arrive too soon', *The Observer* (review), (25 Jan. 1998), p. 8.   25 Power, 'The fine art of surfacing', p. 18.   26 Pettitt, *Screening Ireland*, p. 276.   27 Gerry McCarthy, 'I Went Down' (review), *Film Ireland* (Oct./Nov. 1997), p. 34 and Pettitt,

distinguishable²⁸ and the criminal motifs of the Cork gang are more reminiscent of the western than gangster genre (the Black and Amber bar parallels a
western saloon with Git as 'the stranger' unwelcome in town), there is a sense
of 'placelessness' attached to the cities. Locations are not cosmopolitanized to
resemble an 'anywhere' European city (as in *About Adam* (Gerry Stembridge,
2000) and *Goldfish Memory* (Liz Gill, 2002) or television dramas *Bachelor's
Walk* or *The Big Bow Wow*), but exist as 'non-places'.²⁹ Cork is only identifiable through a title card and Dublin is marginalized to the edge of the narrative, book ending the opening and closing of the film. Instead, the anonymous
bars, motels, back roads and petrol stations take centre stage. It is this lack of
specificity that enables *I Went Down* to exist as a hybrid film. Overtly romantic or metaphorically dark imagery gives way to a blank canvas free from historical and political ideologies allowing the generic conventions of the gangster and road movie to merge freely with the Irish landscape. The traditions
of rural pastoralism are playfully set against the conventions of genre by jux-
taposing the iconography of the gangster genre with rural countryside as when
Bunny and Git, dressed in urban attire, pass through a field filled with cattle.

'DIVORCING JACK' AS A 'HYBRID FILM'

A year subsequent to *I Went Down*, indigenous filmmaking in Northern Ireland
moved away from television drama and the independent low-budget sector
towards a commercial cinema with the release of *Divorcing Jack*. Setting the
standard for the brief surge in what became known as indigenous 'peace-
process' cinema, the film drew on elements of American genre and popular
culture in an effort to differentiate itself from the non-indigenous 'troubles
films' of the past.

    John Hill, in his recent reading of *Divorcing Jack* sees David Caffrey's film
as 'a popular piece of genre filmmaking aimed squarely at the box-office'.³⁰ He
cites influences ranging from Alfred Hitchcock, to Elmore Leonard, Quentin
Tarantino and Danny Boyle's *Trainspotting* (1996). In addition to the influence of popular culture, *Divorcing Jack* follows the Bakhtinian model of merging a variety of Hollywood conventions into a single hybrid form. Set in a
newly independent Northern Ireland of the near future, the narrative concerns
Dan Starkey, a cynical hard-drinking Belfast journalist who begins an affair

Screening Ireland, p. 276. **28** To the point of being undecipherable to American critics such as
Janet Maslin, 'Cavorting in Irish gangland', *New York Times*, section E, (24 June 1998), p. 5.
This could be attributed to colloquialisms (Bunny: 'No guts, no black pudding') as well as enun-
ciation. **29** Anne Scallan, 'Non-places: Irish cinema from another perspective', *Film West*, 32
(May 1998), p. 24. **30** John Hill, '*Divorcing Jack*', in Brian MacFarlane (ed.), *24 Frames: the
cinema of Britain and Ireland* (London, 2005), p. 227.

with a young student, Margaret. Her inexplicable murder and dying words 'Divorce Jack' act as a catalyst for a chain of events that find Starkey on the run from a combined force of the police, various paramilitaries and the first Prime Minister-elect, Michael Brinn. The complex narrative draws upon a diverse range of genres and mixed-genres from romantic-comedy, to thriller, chase-movie, murder-mystery, political conspiracy and black comedy with elements of farce and slapstick, all set amidst the background of 'the troubles'.

The inclusion of an American character, visiting *Boston Globe* journalist Parker who aids Starkey when on the run and acts as a sidekick of sorts, facilitates the use of Hollywood elements. His driving skills instigate a car chase whereby he runs a pursuing loyalist gang off the road, explaining to Starkey: 'I'm from New York. I do this for breakfast'. He is also central in encouraging Starkey to solve the ensuing mystery surrounding the tape and is the unfortunate victim when the plot turns to dark thriller. Other post-modern references relating to genre include the representation of former IRA man Keegan as a suited gangster villain and the sometimes-surreal allusions to the western.[31] One scene that counts the western amongst its many intertextual sources occurs when Starkey is recognized and chased by a gang of loyalist gunmen. This sequence, like the entire film, juxtaposes an outwardly perilous and ultimately violent situation with dark comedy through its use of the theme music from *The Magnificent Seven*. It simultaneously parodies the western, satirises the paramilitaries, and owes a post-modern debt to Tarantino's use of 'Stuck in the Middle with You' from *Reservoir Dogs* (1992). The lampoonish depiction of loyalist warlord Billy McCoubrey, complete in garish country and western attire, destabilizes the traditional representation of Northern Ireland terrorism by highlighting how far removed the terrorists are from the heroic protectors of *The Magnificent Seven*. McLoone comments that the scene 'comes as close as the cinema has ever done to castigating the romantic pretensions of so much paramilitary rhetoric'.[32]

Although clearly comical, this scene illustrates the film's contentious approach of fusing irreverent black humour with serious subject matter. As one reviewer suggested, the use of the words 'comedy' and 'Belfast' in the same sentence strikes an incongruous chord.[33] On the other hand, Dervila Layden argues that comic fiction can play a role in rehabilitating Northern Ireland as a post-traumatic society. Comedy, she contends, 'in creating a distance between the audience and the comic characters, provides a particular type of space where we can imagine a very different world'.[34] She cites *Wild*

31 For more on the western in *Divorcing Jack*, see Hill, '*Divorcing Jack*', p. 233.   32 Martin McLoone, 'Internal decolonisation? British cinema in the Celtic fringe', in Robert Murphy (ed.), *The British Cinema Book*, 2nd edition (London, 2001), p. 185.   33 Ronan Farren, 'A Tarantino touch', *Sunday Independent (Living)* (18 Oct. 1998), p. 31.   34 Dervila Layden, 'Imagining the future: post-Troubles comic fiction', in Kevin Rockett and John Hill (eds), *National cinema and*

about Harry (2000) and the BBC NI/RTE series *Eureka Street* as examples, but this may also apply to *Divorcing Jack* and other 'troubles' comedies such as *Crossmaheart* (1998), *The Most Fertile Man in Ireland* (1999), *With or Without You* (1999), *An Everlasting Piece* (2000) and *Puckoon* (2001). BBC Northern Ireland's comedy series *Give My Head Peace* also successfully merged comedy and politics by creating a cast of over-the-top Nationalist and Unionist characters that satirized and dissected Northern Ireland political culture.

   Divorcing Jack attempts a similar approach but its overt shifts in tone from black comedy to scenes of both brutal and casual violence proves problematic within the context of 'the troubles'. The almost cartoon violence of *The Magnificent Seven* scene sits uncomfortably with the murder of Margaret and the casual way Parker is thrown to his death from a thirteen-story tower block. Taking this hybrid a step further, some deaths are played purely for comic effect. Hill describes how, in following Tarantino, certain scenes display 'a casual disregard towards the taking of life and its emotional consequences',[35] such as when Starkey accidentally kills Margaret's mother by pushing her down the stairs and Lee, the stripping nun-o-gram who rescues Starkey, shoots one of Keegan's men believing her gun to be a replica. The comic-violent hybrid, Hill argues, does not translate to Northern Ireland because 'Tarantino's films occupy a displaced mythic world of popular culture and comic-book violence far removed from the direct experience of its audience' whereas the memory of violence as carried out by paramilitaries in the North is real and still fresh.[36]

   In *Divorcing Jack*, there is evidence to suggest that Northern Irish identity has been hybridized in favour of a new homogenized identity, one that is neither Catholic nor Protestant, British nor Irish. The dominant political party is neither Nationalist or Unionist, but the Alliance lead by a Tony Blair-like Brinn. In the novel, the protagonist Starkey is described as 'a hard drinker and confirmed Unionist'.[37] In the film, however, Starkey's Unionism is diluted to the point of making him, in the words of the director, 'religiously androgynous'.[38] The synopsis on the film's DVD sleeve even goes as far as describing him as 'Irish'. In place of a defined political allegiance, he shows sardonic contempt for both sides of the religious divide and leads a lifestyle inspired by the ethos of 'punk irresponsibility'.[39] In terms of landscape, a hybridity of style is implied, both looking towards the future but simultaneously referencing the past. Martin McLoone describes the film noir-inspired

beyond: studies in Irish film 1 (Dublin, 2004), p. 106.   **35** Hill, '*Divorcing Jack*', p. 232.   **36** Ibid., p. 235.   **37** Colin Bateman, *Divorcing Jack* (London, 1995), p. 8.   **38** Jason Johnston, 'Jack in the Box', *Belfast Telegraph*, (29 Sept. 1998) (accessed from lexis-nexis).   **39** A term first suggested to me by my supervisor Prof. Kevin Rockett. Starkey does, however, make an impassioned but unconvincing speech, not in the novel, at the film's finale about the 'importance of individuals' and the lack of respect the former terrorists have for human life. See Philip Kemp, 'Divorcing Jack', *Sight and Sound*, 8:10 (1998), p. 42 and John Hill, '*Divorcing Jack*', p. 235 for more.

visual style of *Odd Man Out* (1947) as creating Belfast as 'an expressionist city of darkness and fatalistic doom, a dystopian vision of decay rather than recon-struction'.⁴⁰ *Divorcing Jack* was one of the first fiction films to challenge this depiction by replacing the traditional signifiers of place (gantries of Harland and Wolff) and 'troubles' iconography (sectarian murals, barricades and British Army Saracens) with signs of urban prosperity. The streets are full of people and electronic billboards generate a level of interest concerning the upcoming election. Signs of affluence abound as Margaret lives in a spacious, New York-style loft apartment, while Brinn holds a press conference at the Waterfront Hall, a venue that reflects his message of prosperity and new beginnings.

Hill, however, points out that there is 'a central tension within the film between the modern urban realities suggested by the film's settings and the darkness of the film's plot and conclusion'.⁴¹ Juxtaposed alongside this 're-imagined Belfast' remains a Northern Ireland clearly indistinguishable from earlier 'troubles' films. As the narrative becomes darker, so, too, does the topography as Keegan brings a captive Starkey to an imposing, run-down block of flats and later to his home in rural Crossmaheart, a thinly veiled Crossmaglen, complete with barricades, burnt-out cars and bricked-up win-dows. The 'privileging of the pastoral' in Irish cinema identified by Kevin Rockett is reversed in Bateman's vision of Northern Ireland.⁴² Unlike subse-quent new Northern Irish cinema (*With or Without You* and *Wild about Harry*) which presents attractive coastline and rural scenery not seen since *December Bride* (1990), the countryside in *Divorcing Jack* is in keeping with media rep-resentations of South Armagh during the height of the 'troubles'.

CONCLUSION – DOES HYBRIDITY WORK?

I Went Down and *Divorcing Jack* are exemplary of the global filmmaking strate-gies that have been appropriated by Irish filmmakers. The hybridization of genres in both films aim to enhance commercial appeal by tapping into local and global audiences literate in Hollywood genre filmmaking. They both intro-duce a mix of generic elements to an Irish setting, have been compared to a post-Tarantino cycle of gangster film, explore masculinity and the male hero within the 1990s rise of 'laddism',⁴³ stage similar generic set-pieces (car chases,

---

40 Martin McLoone, 'Topographies of terror and taste: the re-imaging of Belfast in recent cinema', Ruth Barton and Harvey O'Brien (eds), *Keeping it real: Irish film and television* (London, 2004), pp 136–7.   41 Hill, '*Divorcing Jack*', p. 230.   42 This is when the 'country' is repre-sented positively as the site of authentic Irishness while the city is deemed a negative space. Kevin Rockett, '(Mis-)Representing the Irish urban landscape', Mark Shiel and Tony Fitzmaurice (eds), *Cinema and the city: film and urban societies in a global context* (Oxford, 2001), p. 217.   43 One reviewer commented on McPherson's recurring fascination with 'the drink-driven excess of lad-culture' and 'the birds and booze lifestyle, which is routinely contrasted with anything

Table 2: *I Went Down* vs. *Divorcing Jack* – Gross and Admissions

	I Went Down (1997)		*Divorcing Jack (1998)*	
Country	Gross	Admissions	Gross	Admissions
Ireland	£IR600,000 (€789,474)	187,500	£IR263,820 (€333,949)	71,302
UK	£578,512 (€863,450)	165,289	£471,483 (€693,357)	125,338
Rest of Europe	€302,358	71,562	€211,184	42,368
USA	$405,297 (€352,432)	98,800	N/A	N/A
Australia	$AUD130,989 (€79,387)	17,486	$AUD252,827 (€160,017)	30,832
Totals	€2,387,101	540,637	€1,398,507	269,840

Sources: European *Audiovisual Observatory's Statistical Yearbooks 1994/1995 – 2003*, The Lumiere Database (http://lumiere.obs.coe.int/web/EN/search.php), *In Production, Variety, Screen Digest*, Ruth Barton, *Irish National Cinema*, 191–2, *Internet Movie Database* (www.imdb.com), the-numbers.com (US only) and moviemarshal.com (Australia only).

Notes: Rest of Europe figures for *Divorcing Jack* include Spain, Italy, Germany and Norway. France, Iceland and Greece are unaccounted for. Other unaccounted territories include New Zealand, South Africa and Japan. Rest of Europe figures for *I Went Down* include Italy, Spain, France, Finland, Belgium and the Netherlands. Unaccounted for territories include Australia, New Zealand and Argentina. Currency Exchange Rates for *I Went Down*: 1997, €1=£IR0.76, $AUD1.65. 1998 €1=£0.67. *Divorcing Jack*: 1998, €1 = £0.68, £IR0.79; 1999, €1 = $AUD1.58 (European Audiovisual Observatory Statistical Yearbook 2003).

shoot-outs and fleeing a hotel) and even employ a Hitchcockian 'MacGuffin' as a catalyst.[44] Both were, in international terms, modesty budgeted and financed through a mixture of television broadcasters, state subsidies and European co-producers.[45] Critically and commercially, *I Went Down* proved more success-

pretentious or middle-class' (Wood, *Conor McPherson*, p. 14). The same can be said of Bateman's novels and screenplays. There are also similarities between Dan Starkey and the narrator in McPherson's *Rum and Vodka*, both of whom are married men whose alcohol-fuelled reckless-ness leads to infidelity with a young student.   **44** In *Divorcing Jack*, 'Divorce Jack' is actually 'Dvořák', a classical music tape given by Margaret to Starkey containing an incriminating record-ing of Brinn confessing his terrorist past. In *I Went Down*, plates for printing counterfeit twenty-dollar bills bring gangsters French and Grogan together along with Bunny and Git for a show-down in the woods.   **45** *Divorcing Jack*, at £3million, was the most expensive indigenous film made in Northern Ireland at that time and was funded by BBC Films, the UK National Lottery, Winchester Films (sales agent) and French co-producer Ima Films. *I Went Down* cost a more modest £IR1.8m with funding from BBC Films, the Irish Film Board, RTE and Euskal Media (prize money won by Breathnach at Spain's San Sebastian Film Festival for *Alisa*).

ful than *Divorcing Jack*. *I Went Down* was well-received by critics at home and abroad and, when on limited released in New York, it met with an over-whelmingly positive response in the print media.[46] In comparison, the response to *Divorcing Jack* was more mixed. Some commentators, including Brian McIlroy, welcomed the film's representation of Protestants and Northern Ireland and applauded its 'willingness to play with clichés in a tense political situation'.[47] Others, however, deemed it tasteless and offensive.[48] Although both films performed poorly internationally, *I Went Down* was the more successful of the two. It earned close to double *Divorcing Jack*'s approximated worldwide gross and, at the Irish box-office, it became the most successful indigenous independent film at that time, grossing £IR600,000.[49] It also received distrib-ution in the United States, which *Divorcing Jack* failed to achieve.

The relative failure of the films internationally suggests that the comic-violent hybrid, as found when elements of the thriller, the chase movie and/or the gangster film are merged with comedy, can be problematic in an Irish set-ting, particularly when social and political elements remain. Emer Rockett defends the hybrid gangster-comedy *Ordinary Decent Criminal* (2000) on the grounds that it achieves a heightened level of reality, a 'hyperreality' that rejects realism and the authentic.[50] However, whereas *I Went Down* avoids contem-porary Irish social issues such as drugs or the paramilitaries,[51] *Divorcing Jack* is weighed down by its political baggage which prevents it from achieving this kind of 'hyperreal', or distinctively cinematic, status. Plots involving Republican and Loyalist terrorists as criminals and future political leaders are too close to reality to be accepted in terms of a purely cinematic space. Therefore it is not that hybridity is unsuited to Irish cinema, but that the landscape must remain free from the realities of social commentary for a multi-generic hybrid film to become fully accepted.

I Went Down's lack of commercial success outside of Ireland does, of course, complicate this issue further. In this case, the film's lack of recogniz-able signifiers of 'Irishness' (in terms of character, landscape and iconography) may have limited its appeal for the larger Irish diaspora. Interestingly in France, the film was re-titled 'Irish Crime', possibly motivated by a belief that an increased awareness of the film's nationality would widen its potential audi-ence. This does not, however, imply that the 'hybrid film' in the context of

---

46 See *Irish Times* (Sound & Vision) (3 Feb. 1998), p. 13.   **47** Brian McIlroy, 'Challenges and problems in contemporary Irish cinema: the Protestants', *Cineaste* (Contemporary Irish cinema supplement), 14: 2–3 (1999), p. 60.   **48** Alexander Walker, 'Divorced from any sense of reality', *Evening Standard* (1 Oct. 1998), p. 26; Nigel Andrews, '*Divorcing Jack* – Review', *Financial Times* (1 Oct. 1998), p. 20.   **49** Maslin, 'Cavorting in Irish gangland', p. 5. Its 'independence', though, can be questioned by the involvement of a major British financier, BBC Films.   **50** Emer Rockett, '*Ordinary Decent Criminal*', in MacFarlane (ed.), *24 Frames*, pp 239–48.   **51** An early draft of the script had a vigilante group connected with the paramilitaries kidnap and assault Git (McPherson et al., *I Went Down*, p. 109). A similar scene can be found in *The General*.

Irish cinema should be avoided. Richard Kearney, for example, warns of the dangers for Irish culture in denying the influence of cosmopolitanism and wider global cultures:

> For as long as Irish people think of themselves as Celtic Crusoes on a sequestered island, they ignore not only their own diaspora but the basic cultural truth that cultural creation comes from hybridisation not purity, contamination not immunity, polyphony not monologue.[52]

By abandoning an 'obsession with an exclusive identity', he suggests, Irish art can achieve both an Irish and international identity. An 'Irish hybrid film', therefore, has the potential to add to the complexity and diversity of 'screen Irishness'. However as the contrasting examples of *I Went Down* and *Divorcing Jack* have illustrated, such hybridity should not be over-reliant on any single foreign cinema, in this case Hollywood, and should seek to transform, and not just copy, the materials it borrows.

52 Richard Kearney, *Postnationalist Ireland: politics, culture, philosophy* (London, 1997), p. 101.

Part 3: Film and Cultural Identity

American dreams and Irish myths: John Sayles' *The Secret of Roan Inish*

PÁDRAIC WHYTE

John Sayles' 1994 film *The Secret of Roan Inish* offers a complex multi-layered representation of myth and folklore that intertwines aspects of a cultural and a personal past. In exploring the relationship between ideas of a mythic past and a modern present, Sayles interweaves concepts of both Ireland and childhood as sites of origin in a contemporary global culture. By positioning the production and reception of the film within diverse theories of globalization this essay draws upon the work of Roland Robertson and concepts of 'glocalization'.[1] Robertson analyses the relationship between the local and the global and the 'global institutionalization of the expectation and construction of local particularism'[2], exploring the complex relationship between issues of universalism and particularism.[3] Such an approach allows for an examination of Sayles' construction of Ireland as a particular site of mythic origins in a film that attempts to speak to the global viewer in universal terms.

Central to this analysis is the significance of transferring the original narrative, *Child of the Western Isles*, a 1957 novella by Rosalie K. Fry, from a Scottish to an Irish setting. This transfer results in the creation of a particular site of origin in the form of Ireland and the subsequent use of concepts of Ireland to explore universal myths for a global audience. It is this relationship of particularism and universalism which creates a methodological framework for the examination of the film. Following Fredric Jameson's suggestion that globalization 'alternately masks and transmits cultural or economic meanings',[4] the global elements of the production process will first be identified.

In Britain the novel was published as *Child of the Western Isles* while in the US it can be found under the title *The Secret of Ron Mor Skerry* (1959). During

---

1 Roland Robertson, 'Glocalization: time-space and homogeneity-heterogeneity', in Mike Featherstone, Scott Lash and Roland Robertson (eds), *Global modernities* (London, 1995). 2 Ibid., p. 38. 3 The concept of 'universalism' is somewhat problematic as it often presumes that diverse cultures around the world experience similar needs and wants, as is found in the work of Joseph Campbell. His work traces the parallel motifs and structures that exist in many cultural myths that originate from contrasting societies. Such an analysis of universalism is beyond the scope of this essay. In essence, it is not necessary for the reader to accept theories of universalism as I simply argue that Sayles is *striving* for a universal myth; whether universalism exists or not is secondary. 4 Frederic Jameson in Frederic Jameson and Masao Miyoshi (eds), *The cultures of globalization* (Durham, NC, 1998), p. 55.

67

World War II, author Fry worked as a coast-watcher in Scotland, where she witnessed seals in their natural habitat and became familiar with the selkie folklore of Scotland.[5] Originally from Canada, Fry draws upon these selkie myths and incorporates them into a narrative that explores the contemporary concerns of a young character named Fiona McConville. While Fry set her story in the contemporary Western Isles of Scotland of 1957, Sayles relocated the narrative to the early 1950s and shot the film on the Donegal coast. The global nature of the production is apparent from the outset; an Irish-American director adapts a novel set in Scotland and written by a Canadian author, relocates the narrative to the north-west Irish coast and receives funding from an American television corporation, Jones Entertainment.[6]

Set in the early 1950s, the plot of *The Secret of Roan Inish* focuses on the experiences of Fiona Coneely[7], a ten year-old girl who leaves her father (Dave Duffy) in the city to live with her grandparents, Hugh and Tess (Mick Lally and Eileen Colgan), and her cousin Eamon (Richard Sheridan), on the Donegal coast.[8] This move from the urban centre to the rural coastline prompts a series of storytelling episodes in which Fiona and consequently the viewer learn about the Coneely family history, in terms of their recent and distant pasts. Four years previously the entire Coneely family were evacuated from their island of Roan Inish, or 'Seal Island', and moved to the mainland. On that day, Fiona's younger brother Jamie was taken out to sea by seals and disappeared. The story focuses on Fiona's quest to uncover the secrets of her family history, find her brother, and live again on Roan Inish. This leads to a search for a sense of identity and understanding in her life, and Fiona discovers that one of her ancestors, Nuala (Susan Lynch), was in fact a selkie woman, a seal who could take the shape of a human. Throughout these stories, Sayles combines elements of realism and fantasy to explore ideas of relating the past to the present, of connecting with nature, and of tracing the function of myth in the modern world.

The relocation of Sayles' narrative from Scotland to Donegal may initially appear insignificant, as selkie folklore is a part of both Irish and Scottish culture and consequently both locations act as credible backdrops to such a

---

5 See John Sayles in John Sayles and Gavin Smith, *Sayles on Sayles* (London, 1998), p. 208. 6 Jones Entertainment is a Colorado-based cable TV corporation. See Paddy Barrett, '*The Secret of Roan Inish*', *Screen International*, 917 (13 July 1993), p. 16.   7 The change of surname from McConville in the novel to Coneely in the film is significant in constructing a specifically Irish dimension to this personal history as the Irish family name 'Coneely' claims selkie origins. The story of the Coneely family and the seals is established in Irish folkloric tradition. See David Thomson, *The people of the sea* (Edinburgh, 1996, orig. 1954), pp 190–1. The tale can be read online at www.irishsealsanctuary.ie/html/folklore. Accessed 06/04/05.   8 In the original novella, Fiona's grandparents reside on one of the larger islands. In the film, this move to the mainland affects the interpretation of the narrative as the story no longer simply deals with island culture, but also explores Irish mainland culture.

tale. This can also be read in terms of Sayles' desire to portray myths that transcend ideas of national boundaries in a global culture, similar to Celtic myths that are found in different nations. David Thomson's *The People of the Sea* (1954) documents many of the shared selkie myths of Ireland and Scotland, several of which Sayles incorporates into Fry's basic narrative structure, thus adding a more complex dimension to the text.[9] However, the deliberate transfer of the narrative setting becomes an important component of constructing themes of origins for a global viewer. The ideological construction of Ireland in cinema throughout the twentieth century means that 1950s Ireland in the film not only functions as a backdrop to events but as an important cultural signifier of themes of loss and return.

Sayles remarks that a number of factors influenced his decision to locate the narrative in Ireland. Along with a greater familiarity with Irish rather than Scottish history, it was the association of concepts of Ireland with ideas of loss that informed his view of the setting:

> [O]ne of the things that I did get from the Irish Americans around me growing up and in Boston was that so many American songs are about going on the road, going to a great place, while Irish songs very often are about loss, they're about leaving something behind. That sense of Ireland being this island that's obsessed with loss – their national sovereignty, their language, their sons and daughters, and a certain past, seemed to me perfect for this particular story, which is about the loss of an island and a way of life. And is there any way to go back to that world? Scotland has its own preoccupations, but the loss isn't as heavy.[10]

The Irish-American community that Sayles refers to is important in understanding both the production and reception of the film in global culture. It can be argued that many of the motifs of origins and homeland that permeate the text appeal to members of the Irish diaspora around the world as Ireland is established as a site of nostalgia. Ireland in the film can be read in John Urry's terms, as a place or a homestead that can be visually consumed.[11]

This approach also relies upon establishing recognizable characteristics of Ireland so that the location and its cultural resonance are immediately identifiable for the global viewer, particularly in terms of land, nationality and Catholicism.[12] However, in using Irish culture and storytelling in order to pro-

---

9 These elements include references to Teach Duinn, the story of Sean Michael and the cingulum, the rescue of Sean Michael, and the story of Liam and the selkie woman.   10 John Sayles in *Sayles on Sayles*, pp 209–10.   11 John Urry, *Consuming places* (London, 1994), p. 1.   12 Fintan O'Toole claims that 'Daniel Corkery's famous definition of Irishness as characterized by Land, Nationality and Catholicism remained ideologically potent right into the 1970s' in *The*

pose a need for myth in contemporary society, Sayles has been criticized by Irish reviewers and academics. Martin McLoone claims that the film succumbs to stereotypical images of romantic Ireland and that it partakes of an 'essentially regressive ideology'.[13] Similarly, Ruth Barton argues that *The Secret of Roan Inish* revisits traditionally conservative and often clichéd representations of Ireland as she aligns the film with *Into the West* (Mike Newell, 1990), claiming that both 'are distinguished by a deep investment in whimsy'.[14] A viewing of the trailer would probably suggest that McLoone and Barton are right. In this montage sequence, Ireland and childhood are imbued with a sense of nostalgia and sentiment as they become a commodified part of the international film industry. The images incorporate the touristic gaze into the narrative as Ireland is represented as 'a rural utopia, to be sold as a commodity to a world market'.[15] This portrayal of a romantic rural Irish landscape may be found in many films from Sidney Olcott's Kalem company films in 1910–12 to Ron Howard's *Far and Away* (1992). In varying ways film depictions of Ireland romanticize the landscape whether it is in terms of 'hard' or 'soft' primitivist representations as discussed by Luke Gibbons.[16] Similar to the portrayal of landscape, the fantasy elements of the film, which fuse myth and magic, are part of a long filmic tradition that associates Ireland with such tropes. This is particularly evident in children's films or family films set in Ireland that often couple a romanticization of the landscape with elements of folklore and magic, as is evident in *Darby O'Gill and the Little People* (1959), *Shamus* (1959), *The Johnstown Monster* (1971), and *Flight of the Doves* (1971). Similarly, the trailer for *Roan Inish* conforms to such romanticization as it concludes with a shot of Fiona saying 'It's a lovely story', a marketing strategy that reinforces the sentimentalization of both Ireland and childhood in the film. As a result, it is possible to read *The Secret of Roan Inish* as a product of a global consumer industry where Ireland is established as a particular local site that is different from the rest of the world. The touristic gaze suggests that the film is not specifically aimed at an Irish audience but at a global viewer. This is quite simply because 'diversity sells'.[17]

   Although elements of the film may adhere to stereotypical representations of Ireland, the dismissal of the film as mere 'whimsy' overlooks the complex layering of a text that centres on the search for origins in a modern world. Given the film's release in 1994 it could be argued that Sayles was a victim of timing. The negative reception[18] of the film in Ireland is part of a much

Ex-Isle of Erin: images of a global Ireland (Dublin, 1996), p. 15.   13 Martin McLoone, *Irish film: the emergency of a contemporary cinema* (London, 2000), p. 211.   14 Ruth Barton, *Irish national cinema* (London, 2004), p. 151.   15 McLoone, *Irish film*, p. 201.   16 Luke Gibbons, 'Romanticism, realism and Irish cinema' in Kevin Rockett, Luke Gibbons and John Hill, *Cinema and Ireland* (London, 1988).   17 Robertson, 'Glocalization', p. 29.   18 See also Janette Hamill's critical review of the film in *Film Ireland*, 41 (June/July 1994). Hamill compares *The Secret of*

larger development in Irish culture and economy from the mid-1990s in the form of the Celtic Tiger.[19] It is important to note that during the period two significant conflicting factors arose in relation to the Irish film industry in terms of economics and of culture. On the one hand, in conjunction with establishing itself as a tourist destination, Ireland introduced further and more attractive tax incentives to encourage foreign filmmakers to shoot on location in Ireland.[20] Secondly, in contrast to this process, many cultural critics and filmmakers were seeking representations of a modern Ireland that dispelled the romantic myth of rural Ireland and favoured the growth of a more socially-conscious tradition in contemporary filmmaking.[21] As a result, any prospect of a return to an inward-looking, culturally-essentialist past was perceived to be at odds with the modern and cosmopolitan, if surface, world of the Celtic Tiger years.

However, it is not the *real* Ireland that Sayles attempts to explore in the film, but an *idea* of Ireland. As many commentators have noted, this idea of loss and return in Ireland, which Sayles draws upon, is epitomized in John Ford's *The Quiet Man* (1952).[22] Sean Thornton's return to the Irish homestead is bound up with a sense of fantasy and wonder and its resonance in relation to homecoming is such that it is later adopted as an intertextual reference in Steven Spielberg's *ET*. It is watching *The Quiet Man* on television that prompts ET's request to 'phone home'. Not only does this oft-cited example establish the significance of *The Quiet Man* as connected to ideas of 'home' but also links the text to the children's film industry and concepts of childhood and origins. Fiona's journey home can be compared to that of Sean Thornton in the form of returned emigrant. The greeting of Fiona by her grandfather is reminiscent of the moment that Sean Thornton encounters Innisfree, his family homestead. Fiona's journey to her grandparents' home can therefore be read as that of the returned emigrant, coming back to discover her roots.

The opening shots of Fiona on board the ferry reverse the traditional image of the emigrant leaving Ireland on board a ship as is evident in films such as *Far and Away* (1992) and *Titanic* (1997). Fiona, positioned at the helm

Roan Inish to the much darker selkie short film *Conneely's Choice* (Barra de Bhaldraithe, 1992) which is based upon the same selkie myths as Sayles' film.   19 See Peadar Kirby, Luke Gibbons and Michael Cronin (eds), *Reinventing Ireland: culture, society and global economy* (London, 2002). 20 McLoone, *Irish film*, p. 201. In the case of *The Secret of Roan Inish*, it is not clear whether or not the production received funding in the form of tax breaks. Paddy Barrett notes that 'Renzi [the producer] tried to access Irish finance via the country's tax breaks for film investors but found the rules too complex and the economy on a downturn' in 'The Secret of Roan Inish', p. 16.   21 McLoone, *Irish film*, p. 203.   22 See Luke Gibbons, *The Quiet Man* (Cork, 2002), Barton, *Irish national cinema*, pp 71–6, McLoone, *Irish film* and Barry Monahan, 'Deconstructing the nation: the Abbey Theatre and stage-Irishness on screen, 1930–1960' (PhD thesis, Trinity College Dublin, 2004).

of the ferry, represents a return to the area that she left approximately four
years ago. During this sequence the audience are provided with a flashback of
Fiona's past as she remembers her mother's funeral on the island of Roan
Inish. The camera pans across the many gravestones on the island, signifying
both the life that once existed and the death that has replaced it. It symbolizes
not only the mortal death of the individual, but also the end of a culture and
way of life on the island which, as is revealed later in the film, is caused by
emigration and mass evacuation. In this sense Ireland's cultural past of emigration, while not directly explored on screen, is implied in the narrative.[23]
Therefore, the emigrant or the subsequent generations in the Irish diaspora
viewing the film are implicated in the opening images in terms of leaving, but
also in terms of returning in search of origins as is represented by the character of Fiona. These images are also aligned with the concept of childhood
as a site of origin, as childhood becomes a commodity for the global viewer.

The problem lies not with Sayles' representation of Ireland, but with his
depiction within the broader context of cultural representations of the nation.
This is the challenge faced by many directors who attempt to document forms
of rural Ireland for a contemporary audience.[24] In a cultural climate that wants
to break from traditional images of the rural in favour of urban-realist depictions of modern Ireland, Sayles' film was bound to meet with criticism. Indeed,
here lies the basic dilemma: while Sayles utilizes established concepts of Ireland
to explore the idea of myth, he becomes implicated in the very tradition of
stereotyping from which he draws. As a result, in terms of reception theory,
many critics have read the use of local images as part of a global tradition of
sentimentalizing Ireland and have failed to acknowledge the subsequent sub-
version of many of these tropes during the course of the narrative.

Due to this complex multi-layered nature of the production, Ireland in
the narrative can be read from both a global and a national perspective.
Although drawing upon established tropes of Ireland to create the narrative
framework, ideas of romantic Ireland are subsequently complicated by the text.
This is revealed by Fiona's journey westward. Having identified Ireland as a
site of nostalgia for a global (or primarily an Irish-American) audience, the
film also acts as a site for the complication of the 'myth of the west' within
Irish culture. Fiona's move from the urban to the rural can initially be read
in terms of the Gaelic nationalist romantic traditions that idealized the west
and rural Ireland in opposition to the industrialized urban centres. This is

23 Terence Brown discusses these radical changes in Irish society noting that 'predominant
amongst these was the widespread rejection of rural life that in the immediate post-war period
quickened into what almost amounted to an Irish exodus' in *Ireland a social and cultural history, 1922–85*, 2nd edition (London, 1987), p. 211.   24 This also poses the questions as to whether
it is possible to portray a rural Ireland that escapes established tropes of filmic representations of
the nation.

established by the initial flashback sequence of the film. As Fiona searches for her father she goes into a busy factory and into a pub. The people in the bar comment upon Fiona's unhealthy appearance, thus suggesting that the city and even modernization are bad for her health. These images of confined spaces are juxtaposed to the open landscapes and seascapes that dominate the rest of the film. At one stage, Hugh also expresses his dislike for the city by saying that it is 'nothing but noise and dirt and people that's lost their senses – couldn't tell the difference between a riptide and a raindrop if you shoved their face in the water'. However, this simplistic binary of urban versus rural is subsequently subverted.

Although Tess laments the fact that 'the east is our future and the west is our past' the traditional myth of the Irish west as rural idyll is not sustained throughout the text. This is evident in the character's constant longing to return to the island. Fiona's cousin Eamon wishes to move back when he gets older; Fiona hopes that she will find Jamie there; while Hugh even notes that the cow produces better milk when on the island. In particular, rural Ireland is not imbued with a community spirit embedded in traditional values that are uncorrupted by progress and industrialization. The rural mainland does not feature as a utopia for the Coneely family. Fiona's grandparents have a desire to leave the Donegal countryside and return to Roan Inish, but they feel that such a wish is unrealistic as there is nobody left on the island and they are too old to live on their own. As a result, they try to survive on the rural west coast with the 'penny pinching' shopkeepers and the inhospitable landlord that wants them out of the house in order to rent it as a summer home to a wealthy family from overseas.[25] Therefore, to apply a dichotomy of modern–urban versus traditional–rural to the film is to reduce the complexity of the text. In a reaction to the processes of modernization, the Coneelys want neither modern Ireland nor traditional Ireland, but something that precedes Catholic nationalist Ireland. This is present in the form of Roan Inish, a place that the film tells us is 'between land and sea', steeped in the Celtic folklore of selkie myths, a folklore that later becomes a reality when the seals return Jamie, the lost child.

In proposing such an interpretation of the film it is useful to draw upon Martin McLoone's reading of *The Kinkisha* (Tommy McArdle, 1977) which explores an old ritual in rural Ireland. The film, set in rural Cavan, focuses on the character of Margaret (Barbara MacNamara) whose baby is born at Pentecost. According to superstition, the child will either kill or be killed unless a robin is crushed to death in the baby's hand. Margaret, caught in a loveless and oppressive relationship, eventually captures the bird and performs the ritual after consulting the local priest. McLoone notes that 'her acting-out of

25 Again, this signifies the impact of globalization on the rural community, specifically in the form of the tourist industry. It is also an allusion to Ireland's colonial history of absentee landlords.

74   *Pádraic Whyte*

a superstitious ritual releases her from the stifling conformity of rural Ireland – she emerges from tradition into modernity by enacting an even older tradition'.[26] The pagan belief and ritual gives Margaret a source of empowerment that is not offered by either Catholicism or modernity. A similar process occurs in *The Secret of Roan Inish* as the Coneelys reject both the traditions of the rural mainland and the modernity of the city in favour of the Celtic folklore of the island, an act which empowers Fiona and gives her the determination to find Jamie.

The film can be placed within the cultural context of a moment when Ireland was faced with the onset of a rapid modernization process. Released in 1994, the same year that the term 'Celtic Tiger' was coined, the film may be understood as a transitional text. It represents a moment of change where 'society displays an odd mixture of progressive and reactionary elements'[27] with different alternatives competing for a place in the new Ireland. In essence, it is not just a choice between traditions of Catholic Ireland or modernizing globalization; there is also a possibility of the rejection of both in favour of elements of an older tradition and way of life. The film suggests that the answers to modern-day ills do not lie in the myths of the Irish west, but somewhere beyond the west coast, a liminal space where myths are part of the reality of living. Sayles repeatedly proposes the value of incorporating myth and storytelling into daily life, echoing Joseph Campbell's belief that 'myths are a function of nature as well as of culture, and as necessary to the balanced maturation of the human psyche as is nourishment to the body'.[28]

This also corresponds to Eugene Halton's view that the decline in myth has accompanied a culture of global capitalism, where the rise of capitalism is 'associated with the rise of individualism and the breakdown of traditions as binding forces in society'.[29] Halton argues that a return to myth will give people a sense of identity and a means of coping with the modern world. In *Roan Inish*, the alternative to globalization is present in the form of Celtic myths and folklore that are continually referred to as 'superstition' but which have a very real part to play in the lives of the Coneelys. It is only through the child protagonist Fiona that the older characters in the film can gain access to their own folkloric traditions and island origins.

Consequently, similar to Ireland, constructions of childhood in the film are also aligned with ideas of origin as the child character is employed as a means of rediscovering the family's past, corresponding to Valerie Krips' con-

26 McLoone, *Irish film*, p. 103.   27 Ibid.   28 Joseph Campbell, *The flight of the wild gander: explorations in the mythological dimensions of fairy tales, legends, and symbols* (1951, New York, 1990), p. 3.   29 Eugene Halton, 'The modern error: or, the unbearable enlightenment of being' in Mike Featherstone et al. (eds), *Global modernities*, p. 264. Halton argues that in 'the virtual reality of consumption culture anything goes if people will buy it, only the real cost for the delusion of endless possession is a loss of self-possession' (p. 272).

cept that 'the child is in fact the ultimate conduit to the past, representing not only the most intimate past of self, but the past of culture as well'.[30] This is evident through the series of storytelling episodes that connect Fiona to the lives of her ancestors. Storytelling operates as a major feature in the text as Fiona is told tales of her ancestors who fought the British; Liam Coneely taking the selkie woman Nuala for his wife; and the tragic events on the day the island was evacuated and her brother Jamie drifted out to sea.

The fusion of personal and cultural identity is signified through these various episodes of storytelling as Fiona's quest for knowledge helps to re-ignite the Coneelys' interest in their family history. Initially, her grandparents are reluctant to tell Fiona about the reality of the selkie myths and folklore. As the adults are hesitant to believe in the truth of the tales, Fiona's unrelenting interest results in the association of folklore with the realm of childhood. It is left to her mysterious cousin Tadhg to explain the true events of the family's selkie origins. Although an adult, Tadhg is described as child-like, 'a bit special' and as a 'troubled soul caught between air and water'. It is this childlike quality that allows Tadhg to believe in the fantasy world of selkies, aligning him with Fiona. From this moment onward Fiona tries to convince her grandparents and her cousin Eamon that there is some truth to the selkie myths and that her brother Jamie is still alive (Fiona has seen Jamie). The teenager Eamon is easily persuaded as he too is close to the childhood realm and in turn close to nature and the myths it contains, commenting that 'there's some tales that's true'. However, as Fiona pursues her quest to uncover the secrets of the island Tess soon comes to realise the value of believing in the myth as they return to the island to find Jamie.

It is significant to note the generation gap which exists in the film. While Fiona's father represents a particular generation's disbelief in the myths and the potential that the island still holds as supporting a way of life, Hugh and Tess signify the last remaining traces of a generation that once lived with myth as part of their everyday lives. The grandparents are reluctant to agree that it is possible to return to the island and live as they once did. It is only through Fiona and Eamon's persistence that they slowly become convinced. The younger generation of children aid in bringing new life to the myths of the island, a revived hope that forces the older generation to realise the value and importance of the stories and a closeness to nature that they are trying to suppress. This idea is reinforced during Fiona's conversation with Tadhg as he says 'welcome back Fiona Coneely, we've been waiting'. During this sequence, Fiona is established as having a deeper understanding of her family's history and also a strong link to her ancestors. In the story that Tadhg recounts it is revealed that Fiona Coneely was also the name of the Nuala's eldest daugh-

---

30 Valerie Krips, *The presence of the past: memory, heritage, and childhood in postwar Britain* (New York, 2000), p. 24.

ter, directly connecting Fiona to her selkie past. The comment also signals a form of expectation in Fiona's return, a child who can gain access to the ancestral folklore and help recover the child Jamie who signifies the physical manifestation of the family's loss.

At various moments in the film the child characters, and those who are childlike, are connected with the sea, the landscape, and the wildlife, a feature that dominates many children's films. This alignment of childhood and nature is evident on a number of occasions such as Fiona's drifting across the sea to Roan Inish, Eamon's seafaring capabilities, Tadhg's ability to catch fish with his bare hands, and Jamie's adoptive guardians as seals. The ancestral link to the selkies also connects the family to nature, with both Jamie and Tadhg described as 'dark ones', their dark eyes originating from the seal branch of the family. The selkie stories are bound up with ideas of humans working in conjunction with nature, as opposed to destroying it, where, as Tadhg notes, 'man and beast lived side by side sharing the wealth of the sea'. This corresponds to Eugene Halton's theories that '[i]t is time to begin to body forth a new world view and world civilization, new ways of living both locally and globally in harmony both with nature and the nature within us ... as well as rediscovering the lost resources of the human past and new ways of joining them to the present'.[31] Once again, it is possible to read this as Sayles' attempt to remind the modern viewer of the value of returning to a life that is in harmony with nature.

Throughout these sequences there is a sense that the child knows something much more than adults and has access not only to a different world, but to a different perspective of the world. In Marina Warner's terms, 'the child both mirrors our potential and represents what we have forfeited', recovering something that the majority of adult characters have lost.[32] Childhood, like Ireland, is not a realistic representation but an imagined idea that is used to explore links with a mythic past. The association of childhood with the other worlds of myth and folklore is a common trait in many stories. As Warner notes, 'the commitment of the Romantics to imagination, to fantasy as an instrument of truth, led them to this idea of the child who could provide an unspoiled, undoctored, spontaneous response to the world'.[33] This is how the child character is represented in Sayles's text, and functions as a means of bridging the real world and the world of fantasy. It is this contemporary child mythology that 'presupposes that the child has access to a form of desirable wisdom, of potent innocence'.[34] Sayles uses the idea of the child to reveal the audience's loss of understanding of the world and of nature. Only through these figures can the spectator gain access to these myths of origin. The child

---

31 Halton, 'The modern error', p. 276.   32 Marina Warner, *Cinema and the realms of enchantment* (London, 1993), p. 41.   33 Ibid., p. 40.   34 Marina Warner, *Managing monsters: six myths of our time* (London, 1994), p. 36.

protagonist therefore provides a dual narrative function in the film. The character of Fiona as hero can appeal to younger viewers as her knowledge of the reality of the myth places her in a privileged position to the adult characters. Meanwhile, she also represents a site of memory and loss for the adult spectator. However, this sense of loss is coupled with themes of hope.

Eamon and Fiona's restoration of the cottages represents a new beginning on the island, and it is possible to read the return to Roan Inish as a combination of both the myth of the Irish west and the American west. There is a move westward, to an old heartland, but one that has the potential for new beginnings. This is evident in Fiona's comment to Eamon as she stands by her mother's grave on the island: 'We'll plant some things here when we move back', recognizing the death of one form of life on the island, but also the ability to forge a new future for herself that will draw upon tradition but will not necessarily be confined by it. As the film concludes, Eamon, Fiona, Jamie and their grandparents sit in the newly renovated cottage on Roan Inish. Jamie, as a feral child uncorrupted by the modern world, may be read as a form of hope, a *tabula rasa*, where this small community can create a new and alternative way of life.

It is the belief in myth and ritual, however, along with working in harmony with nature that has led to Jamie's return. Myth and storytelling are present in the film in several forms. The tales to which the child Fiona is exposed create a larger story of the film narrative for the global viewer. The particular elements of selkie lore and Ireland are constructed in a form that attempts to appeal to the viewer on a universal scale as a reminder of the existence of alternatives to a modern global society. The spectator is encouraged to parallel Fiona's journey by using myth and storytelling in the creation of identity and understanding in contemporary society. This conforms to Campbell's idea that myths

> are the world's dreams. They are archetypal dreams and deal with great human problems. I know when I come to one of these thresholds now. The myth tells me about it, how to respond to certain crises of disappointment or delight or failure or success. The myths tell me where I am'.[35]

Sayles also appeals to the viewer to find his/her way in the world by using myth.

In establishing a sense of home and origin, Sayles draws upon a series of international texts in the creation of the film, localizing the narrative and events in an attempt to explore universal myths of origins in a global culture and to renegotiate the position of myth in the modern world. He presents the viewer with a possible alternative to capitalist consumerism, but perhaps that possi-

---

35 Joseph Campbell, *The power of myth* (New York, 2001, orig. 1988), p. 15.

bility is also lost and can never be retrieved. The film ends with a group of people who cannot procreate and therefore will reach an inevitable end in their alternative realm.[36] For the Irish viewer, there is a sense that a modern and globalized Ireland is unavoidable. While the film offers the possibility of an alternative, perhaps this can only ever be a form of cinematic escapism, an imaginary landscape, a fleeting moment of fantasy that ultimately can never become a reality.

As a result, the themes of origin that are created in the film can only ever occupy an imagined space. On screen, the home that is Ireland and the past that is childhood do not exist in reality, but as Warner suggests in relation to homecoming in myth, 'the imaginary homeland itself is homeless. There is no home except in the mind, where ideas of home are grown … home as a place or time of innocence can only be an illusion'.[37] Therefore, representations of childhood and of the Irish past do not attempt to achieve verisimilitude in the film, but function as modes of accessing a search for origins and for the formation of identity in contemporary culture. It is impossible to return to an authentic Irish past or to a child perspective, but it is the attempt to do so that facilitates the processes of self-discovery.

---

36 This echoes themes of incest, or knowing too much, in Sayles' *Lone Star* (1997).   37 Warner, *Managing monsters*, pp 93–4.

From waste to worth:
the politics of self-sacrifice in *H3*

HISTORICAL CONTEXT

During the course of the twentieth century, Irish political prisoners inter-mittently employed the hunger strike as a form of prison protest. Historically, the hunger strike has fulfilled more of a symbolic than an instrumental function, provoking the historian George Sweeney to observe that its association with 'religio-political martyrdom' and 'the pantheon of Irish heroes' who participated in the hunger strike fortified its symbolic strength.[1] Sweeney describes the prevailing climate at the beginning of the twentieth century as religio-political by alluding to a 'reawakening of both religious practice and nationalism together with a militant republicanism'. He concludes that '[o]ne manifestation of this religio-political fusion was the satisfying of societal and psychic needs through self-sacrifice'.[2] Analogously, self-starvation on the part of prisoners in the Free State and later in the Republic, as well as those held in Northern Irish prisons, has historically been considered in the context of self-sacrifice. Certainly, self-immolation was the pre-eminent method of resisting the extension of state power available to prisoners. For instance, when the Free State government decided to amend the Emergency Powers Act, enabling them to intern suspected terrorists without trial or charge in 1940, instances of Hunger Strike among IRA prisoners in the South escalated.

Admittedly, some instances of self-starvation garnered more recognition than others, even if martyrdom was unreservedly bestowed on all those who endured hunger strike to the death. The Lord Major of Cork in 1920, Terence MacSwiney achieved eminence after he died in Brixton prison on day seven-ty-four of his hunger strike. The recalling of a section from his inauguration speech during the 1981 hunger strike in the H-Block of the Maze Prison indi-cates its political relevance to the H-Block campaign. In this speech, he stated: 'It is not those who can inflict the most, but those who can suffer the most

---

1 George Sweeney, 'Irish hunger strikes and the cult of self-sacrifice', *Journal of Contemporary History* 28:3 (1993), p. 421. 2 Ibid., p. 423. 3 Cain Web Service: The Hunger Strike of 1981 – Summary, viewed at http://cain.ulst.ac.uk/events/hstrike/summary.htm 16/02/05.

who will conquer.'[3] Political prisoners redeployed these words in a calculated effort to extend the parameters of support for their campaign by linking it to a historical struggle for independence, which itself was inextricably bound to the politics of self-sacrifice. By the early 1980s, it had become overwhelmingly obvious that an ability to publicize effectively the act of self-immolation was vital to the success of the prison protest and the prisoner's body became a primary site of socio-symbolic contestation.

Since the early 1970s, the British government had been waging a propaganda war aimed at depoliticizing the republican movement. Terminology borrowed from popular culture, such as 'the Godfathers of crime', became quotidian political parlance during this period and was designed to persuade the larger public of the criminality of militant republicanism. The British government's weaponry however was not limited to rhetoric alone. Aside from participating in a propaganda war, they were responsible for significant legislative changes and, in 1976, the British authorities withdrew the 'special category status' for political prisoners. By abolishing the 'special category status' previously enjoyed by paramilitary prisoners, they nullified the distinction between political and criminal prisoners. This plan conspired to stymie the efforts of IRA prisoners to correlate their struggle with that of their republican forefathers, not least those who died during the 1916 Rising, and to prevent them from projecting themselves as part of a historical continuum to the wider nationalist community.

FILMING THE HUNGER STRIKES

Although the hunger strikes received abundant attention in national and international media of the time, they were never common subjects of popular representation. Due to the unprecedented scale of violence during 'the troubles', representations of the republican movement were commonly held to be apologist, and as such were avoided by organs of the media. The peace process however radically altered the remit of the media and a proclivity for remembering traumatic events became evident in both broadcast and print media. In total, three feature films relating to the hunger strikes *H3* (2001), *Some Mother's Son* (1996) and *Silent Grace* (2000) emerged during the period following the 1994 IRA ceasefire. In addition to a new-found yen for courting previously taboo subjects, the sacrificial motif surfaced in popular representation, as is evident from *H3*. Two decades after the event, and an interlude during which republican prison protests were conspicuously absent from popular formats, *H3* portrays the suffering endured by political prisoners in the Maze prison.

COMMEMORATION

Of course, the incarnation of peace since the Good Friday Agreement in 1998 has encouraged the production of feature films pertaining to violence and loss. For its part, *H3*'s interpretation of these themes enacts a memorial function. According to Gregory Ulmer, memorials function in societies when the losses that they commemorate are recognized as sacrifices on behalf of a public, collective value.[4] The media in Northern Ireland have emerged from the censored environment of the 'troubles' to become a conduit through which the past can, finally, be commemorated. Consequently, *H3* is arguably one of the first popular examples of a peripheral memorial to the H-Block campaigns in audio-visual culture.[5] Ulmer describes the function of 'peripheral' memorials in the US context as ones which 'make a case for losses of life (or other kinds of loss) whose public collective relevance as "sacrifice" is not yet recognized'.[6] Previously, an unwillingness to partake in 'republican propaganda' meant that the sacrificial dimension of certain republican campaigns was avoided in popular representations.

CRITICAL THEORY

H3's narrative trajectory proposes that political prisoners in the H-Blocks of the Maze prison purposefully modulated the significance of their campaigns, notably the dirty protest and the hunger strikes, to instigate the transformation, from waste to worth, of their socio-symbolic status within the prison. As one of the first examples in popular representation to forge a relationship between the self-abjection of prisoners during the dirty protest and the self-sacrifice of the hunger strikers, *H3* shows the squalid living conditions inside the Maze while allowing religious imagery, replete with sacrificial connotations, to infuse its visual narrative. The film's system of signification is established through scenes of nudity that allow themes of both abjection and sacrifice to be inscribed on the actors' bodies. In its foregrounding of the body via scenes that disclose both the prisoners' self-abjection and the abjection imposed upon them by prison officers, *H3* exemplifies some of the characteristics of abjection in narrative representation that have been defined by French psychoanalyst Julia Kristeva. Kristeva isolates a 'crying-out theme of suffering horror' coexisting with 'the incandescent states of a boundary-subjectivity'[7] as indicative of the theme of abjection in representation. By adapting Kristeva's notion of abjection, I will argue that the

---

4 Gregory Ulmer, 'The Upsilom Project', in P. Campbell and A. Kear (eds), *Psychoanalysis and performance* (London, 2001), p. 209.　5 *Silent Grace* (2001) is an analogous example.　6 Ulmer, 'The Upsilom project', p. 209.　7 Julia Kristeva, *Powers of horror: an essay on abjection* (New York, 1982), p. 141.

representation of the prisoners' self-abjection, notably during the dirty protest, does not constitute a mere reactive protest on the part of the prisoners, but rather a concerted effort to disrupt and to forge anew the socio-symbolic order within the prison. Elements of Georgio Agamben's political theory are used to indicate how *H3* represents the disquiet among republican prisoners in response to the British government's attempt to depoliticize their struggle by reducing their socio-ontological status to, what Agamben refers to as, 'creaturely' or 'bare life'.[8] In *H3*, prisoners resist the state's efforts to reduce them to 'bare life' by performing a 'boundary-subjectivity' based on their own abjection, and in so doing they repudiate those normative rules ordinarily obeyed by the disciplined or 'docile' prison body.[9] In addition to applying Agamben's theoretical writing on the governmental administration of bare life to the British state's management of the Northern Irish prison population, I will also correlate his interpretation of the 'sovereign exception'[10] with the 'state of emergency' that has characterized the rule of government in Northern Ireland since its inception, most notably during 'the troubles'. Finally, by referring to René Girard's writing on sacrifice and alluding to references to Christian iconography within the film, I will explicate how the mode of address that is subsequently mobilized constitutes a narrative bias that serves as an antidote to the depoliticizing of the republican struggle during the relevant historical juncture represented within the film.

THE SOVEREIGN EXCEPTION

Walter Benjamin's perspicacious observation that the state of emergency had become the rule in modern states seems an apt summary of the mode of governance operating in Northern Ireland, particularly during the 1970s. An almost interminable 'state of emergency' in the North, in which the security of the state was threatened, provided the British government with the necessary pretext to employ the special powers acts. Widespread abuses of detainees during this period provided alarming confirmation of the biopolitical stakes of the British state's involvement in Northern Ireland. Agamben notes how '[p]lacing biological life at the centre of its calculations, the modern State therefore does nothing other than bring to life the secret tie uniting power and bare life'.[11]

8 Georgio Agamben, *Homo Sacer: sovereign power and bare life homo*, trans. D. Heller-Roazen (Stanford, 1995). For Agamben, the terms 'bare' or 'natural' life designate those who are excluded from the political community and who are regarded not as citizens but as biological or 'creaturely life'. 9 See Michel Foucault, *Discipline and punish: the birth of the prison* (London, 1979). 10 Agamben describes the 'sovereign exception' or the 'state of exception' as 'not the chaos that precedes legal order but the situation resulting from its suspension' in *Homo Sacer*, p. 161. In Northern Ireland, as in other parts of the world, the 'sovereign exception' unveiled itself during internment, sanctioning the exclusion of certain individuals, notably members of the IRA, from the political community. 11 Agamben, *Homo Sacer*, p. 6.

Emergency measures such as internment without trial revealed the 'hidden point of intersection between the juridico-institutional and the biopolitical models of power' in Northern Ireland.[12] Although internment was deemed a political failure and as such was aborted in 1975, the state's efforts to quash the republican movement continued under different guises. Single court judges along with other emergency measures and the criminalizing of political prisoners demonstrated the extension of the state's biopolitical leverage and the diminution of citizens' rights.

It could be argued that *H3*'s representation of the Maze prison corresponds to Agamben's figure of 'the camp',[13] a term which he uses, as both a primary metaphor and concrete example, to describe the administration of human life in western liberal democracies. He selects the Nazi concentration camp as the prototypical example in which individuals, although recognized as human beings, remain excluded from the political community by a state power. Agamben identifies this figure of 'the camp' as 'the pure, absolute, and impassable biopolitical space (insofar as it is founded solely on the state of exception)', adding that it 'will appear as the hidden paradigm of the political space of modernity, whose metamorphoses and disguises we will have to learn to recognize'.[14] As the 'hidden matrix of the politics in which we are still living',[15] he stresses the political urgency of recognizing the camp in all of its 'metamorphoses into the *zones d'attentes* of our airports and certain outskirts of our cities'.[16] 'The Cages' at Long Kesh, erected during internment, embodied this figure of the camp and they were even regarded in international media of the day as comprising a concentration camp. The H-Blocks, a top security prison represented in *H3*, were built on the grounds of Long Kesh and were part of the British government's strategy of normalizing 'the Northern Irish problem' so that republican prisoners would be undifferentiated from ordinary criminals. As a form of political resistance, the prisoners refused to refer to the new penal institution by its official name of HMP Maze, and continued to call it Long Kesh, after the prison camp that had previously occupied the site. In a historical work of the period, one internee remembers a prison officer's rebuke when he dared to recall his citizen's rights, '"Listen, you smarty bastard, under the Special Powers Act we can keep you here as long as we like. You can't see anyone. No one will know where you are and we don't have to charge you with anything. If one of those soldiers happens to shoot you, there'll be no inquest either, you bastard." Having read the SP Acts I knew this to be unfortunately all too true'.[17] The special powers, still in effect during the period in which the film was set, irrevocably shaped the overall context according to which the psychological humiliation and physical degradation of political prisoners is presented within

---

12 Ibid.   13 Ibid., p. 123.   14 Ibid., p. 123.   15 Ibid., p. 175.   16 Ibid.   17 John McGuffin, *Internment* (Tralee, 1973), chap. 8, viewed at: http://www.irishresistancebooks.com/internment/intern8.htm on 06/05/05

the film. *H3*'s representation of a situation in which prisoners were at the mercy of predominantly sadistic prison officers mirrors Agamben's observation that when 'the normal order is de facto suspended and in which whether or not atrocities are committed depends not on law but on the civility and ethical sense of the police who temporarily act as sovereign'.[18]

The temporal coincidence of *H3*'s production with debates regarding terrorism provokes comparison between *H3*'s representation of prisoners and an entity, identified by Slavoj Žižek following 9/11, in which Islamic terrorists are considered as neither enemy soldiers nor common criminals but as 'unlawful combatants'.[19] Although the British government criminalized political prisoners in Northern Ireland, their resolute refusal to interpret their terrorist activities as random acts of apolitical violence[20] implied that they did not, despite the policy of 'normalization', perceive these individuals as ordinary criminals. This argument is further borne out in the British state's subjection of prisoners to disciplinary codes reserved for 'political Enemies, foreclosed from the political space proper'.[21] The violence towards republican prisoners shown in *H3* suggests that the relationship between republican prisoners and the prison officers differs significantly from that of these same officers and ordinary decent prisoners or 'ODCs'. In a scene in which the services of a large contingent of riot police are enlisted, the prisoners are dragged naked from their cells, some already bleeding, while others are shown receiving liberal bashes from a brigade of police officers wielding their signature batons. A scene later, one prisoner is shown sitting naked on the floor of his cell as blood streams from his nose and down his chest. The venting of such violence towards exclusively republican prisoners indicates the distinction from the point of view of the officers between these prisoners and 'ODCs'. One officer who demonstrates civility towards the prisoners, regardless of their creed, is jeered by an officer of lower rank for being a 'provi lover'. When he reprimands this officer by asking him to repeat what he has just stated, the officer in question unrepentantly announces 'I said provi lover sir'. The dutiful officer is presented as being unique in his non-sectarian approach, since the rest of the prison officers express only intense hostility toward the republican prisoners.

STATES OF ABJECTION

H3 represents the collusion between forces of the state in the systematic daily humiliation of republican prisoners.[22] The micro-politics of such psychologi-

---

18 Agamben, *Homo Sacer*, p. 174. 19 Slavoj Žižek, *Welcome to the desert of the real* (London, 2002), p. 93. 20 Likewise the US would refuse to regard terrorist attacks on the US as apolitical while refusing to consider their political motivations. See Žižek, *Welcome to the desert of the real*, p. 93. 21 Ibid.

cal and physical humiliation anticipated the devaluation of the prisoners' political worth. In its exemplification of Agamben's notion of the 'sovereign exception', *H3* illustrates how state authorities capitalized on emergency power measures to treat republican prisoners as instances of 'creaturely' or 'bare life'. Even though an international backlash rendered internment a political failure and *H3* is not set during the relevant historical period, it constituted a preliminary stage in the British government's determination to depoliticize the republican movement, with which the film itself is concerned. There is abundant archival evidence of the dehumanizing treatment of republican prisoners in Northern Irish prisons and detention centres during both internment and the proceeding period. As a site of socio-political formation and/or deformation, the H-Blocks can be likened to Agamben's notion of the 'anthropological machine', a term which he uses to describe 'the onto-political grammar of production of the human against a background of life defined as worthless and eliminable'.[23] In his personal writings, Bobby Sands, an elected MP and leader of the 1981 Hunger Strikes in the H-Blocks, described the animality of living conditions inside the Maze: 'I felt like an animal squatting in the corner of the cell among the rubbish and dirt'.[24] For prisoners who were frequently denied access to writing and reading materials, the intellectual, and therefore human, realm was closed off from them. The criminalizing policy that the British state embarked upon should be considered in a similar context and, moreover, as an example of how specific language usage supplemented the physical degradation of republican prisoners in order to exclude them, if not from the human community, at least from a political one. The prisoners depicted in *H3* resist such political devaluation and human degradation on two fronts: they use their bodies to abject themselves in an effort to unsettle the social order within the prison; they also use the Irish language to inscribe their existence in an alternative symbolic realm. Many republican prisoners learnt the Irish language while they were incarcerated, and the determination of prisoners to speak in a native vernacular is shown in the film through the persistent communication between prisoners in Irish despite the difficulties of many in gaining command of the language. *H3* represents the devaluing of prisoners as operating in both the linguistic and physical domains, while simultaneously revealing the prisoners' methods of resistance as correspondingly diverse.

---

22 The state's toleration of the maltreatment of prisoners has ensured that no British soldier or member of the RUC has been convicted for killing or ill-treating persons in Northern Ireland since 1968. 23 Giorgio Agamben is quoted in a review of his book *The open: man and animal* by Guillermina Seri for an online journal *Politics and Culture*, edited by Amitava Kumar and Michael Ryan, viewed at: http://aspen.conncoll.edu/politicsandculture/page.cfm?key=409 on 9 June 2005. 24 Bobby Sands, *One day in my life* (Cork, 1982), p. 50.

FROM STATE TO SELF-ABJECTION

H3's depiction of the mirror searches, in which prisoners were subjected to
internal searches, invokes a comparison with Lacan's famous 'mirror stage'.
According to Lacanian theory, the mirror stage occurs when the baby sees its
reflection for the first time and forms its 'ideal ego' or self through an imaginary identification with the image of its body. Taking place in the imaginary
realm, the baby confuses its own image for its ideal self and subsequently misrecognition ensues. Forced to lie across a mirror bench, thus magnifying the
specularity of their naked bodies, the prisoners are shown fiercely retaliating
against these procedures. Bullied by officers to lie astride the mirror bench,
it is as though the officers' attempt to restage Lacan's imaginary phase in order
to prompt a reoccurrence of the stage in which misrecognition of the self takes
place. As far as is possible, the prisoners resist the prison officers' direction
of their imaginary identification with the degraded image of their bodies in
the mirror. A later scene echoes a comment made by Maud Ellmann, in the
context of the Maze prison, that 'the spectacle of nakedness titillates the clothed
with the delusion of their own superiority'.[25] In this scene, a prison officer,
who expresses hostility towards the prisoners throughout the film, scrutinizes
McCann as he showers fully naked. At other times during the narrative, when
they are regularly and gratuitously hit with batons, the prisoners' treatment
by prison officers extends far beyond protocol and differs from that of 'ODCs'.
The officers sadistically humiliate the prisoners, one of whom jeeringly asks
during the mirror search: 'Didn't your ma tell you how to wash'. Another
officer taunts him about the illegitimacy of their struggle and their lack of
political status: 'you can forget about the IRA now, there is no army here
except the British army, no officers commanding, except for me and my officers. From now on you are 1844 McCann'. Through words, and later in
actions, McCann resists the officer's attempts to humiliate him. He tells him,
'I won't be wearing the prison uniform or doing prison work, I'm not a criminal, I'm a political prisoner'. In his eventual participation in the dirty protest,
McCann enacts his defiance of the authority wielded by those officers responsible for his humiliation and, by extension, that of the British government.

  Kristeva's understanding of abjection concords with that of George Bataille,
who links it to 'the inability to assume with sufficient strength the imperative
act of excluding'.[26] In *H3*, prisoners reverse this logic of exclusion. Rather than
excluding defilement for fear of the threat it might pose to identity, they
include it. By including rather than excluding filth, the prisoners control their
abjection instead of having it visited upon them through degrading treatment
during procedures such as strip and internal or 'rectal mirror'[27] searches.

25 Maud Ellmann, *The hunger artists: starving, writing and imprisonment* (London, 1993), p. 102.
26 Bataille in Kristeva, *Powers of horror*, p. 64.   27 Sands, *One day*, p. 65.

Kristeva describes the abject as 'what is jettisoned from the "*symbolic system*".
It is what escapes that social rationality, that logical order in which a social
aggregate is based, which then becomes differentiated from a temporary
agglomeration of individuals and, in short, constitutes a *classification system* or
a *structure*'.[28] Similarly, in *H3*, the prisoners' dirty protest disturbs the collective existence of prison life and through their self-abjection, they allow '[e]xcre-
ment and its equivalents (decay, infection, disease, corpse, etc.) stand for the
danger to identity that comes from without: the ego threatened by the non-
ego, society threatened by its outside, life by death'.[29] By actively defiling themselves, the prisoners retaliate against their criminalization and, even more
importantly, disturb the socio-symbolic order within the prison, in turn mit-
igating the exertion of the state's biopower within the prison. Ellmann identifies the strategy adopted by actual prisoners in the Maze of admitting the
abject into the collective life of the prison: 'it was the bowels that provided
the excremental ink with which the inmates autographed their cells, defying
their containment with incontinence'.[30]

   H3 adeptly visualizes stages in the prisoners' self-abjection. In its opening frame, a close-up reveals the protagonist Seamus Scullion, a composite
character, lying naked beneath his blankets while resting his head upon a flat-
tened pillow. As part of their no-wash campaign, prisoners desisted from
having their hair cut and subsequently their unkempt manes became nests for
maggots. Scullion gazes vacantly after a maggot as it sluggishly inches its way
across the bare concrete. A wall smeared in excrement occupies the background
of the shot. Shortly after, two men in gas masks, wearing vivid yellow jump
suits, are directed towards an area that requires fumigating. Further reference
to the protests is made in a scene showing Scullion's cellmate McCann des-
perately in need of the toilet. He paces up and down his cell before Scullion
finally directs him to 'go into the corner and let nature take its course'. A few
moments later, McCann reluctantly tears a piece of sponge from the corner
of his mattress and spreads excrement across the wall. By incorporating filth
into their lives, prisoners are represented as using their own abjection to destabilize the disciplinary mechanisms and symbolic order within the prison.
Kristeva argues that it is not lack of cleanliness or health that causes abjection but 'what disturbs identity, system, order. What does not respect bor-
ders, positions, rules'.[31] As a transgression of a bodily border, the dirty protest
is signified not as the ultimate stage in prisoners' humiliation, but rather as a
radical method of resisting state power. Historically, the dirty protest is perceived as one in which prisoners breached the delimitations of civilized human
behaviour. Indeed, it might be argued that *H3* does not provide a faithful portrayal of the animality into which prisoners on the dirty protest descended.

28 Julia Kristeva, *The portable Kristeva* (New York, 1997), p. 256.   29 Ibid., p. 260.   30 Ellmann,
The hunger artists, p. 105.   31 Kristeva, *Powers of horror*, p. 4.

Although *H3* contains scenes of intense suffering, they do not realise the degeneracy of which Bobby Sands speaks: 'An unwashed body, naked and wrecked with muscular pain, squatting in a corner, in a den of disease, amid piles of putrefying rubbish, forced to defecate upon the ground where the excreta would lie and the smell would mingle with the already sickening evil stench of urine and decaying waste food'.[32] Rather than painstakingly approximating the daily discomfort of life on the blanket and participation in the dirty protest, *H3* summarizes prisoners' traversal of the border separating animal nature from human culture to focus on how they resisted not only their interpellation as criminals through the policy of normalization, but also the wider biopolitical designs of the British state.

FOOD AND ABJECTION

By refusing to exclude defilement from their daily existence, the prisoners threaten the socio-symbolic order of the prison. After visiting the H-Blocks, Cardinal Ó Fiaich reported on cell conditions, 'The stench and filth in some cells, with the remains of rotten food and human excreta scattered around the walls, was almost unbelievable. In two of them I was unable to speak for the fear of vomiting'.[33] In the film, even before the hunger strikers begin their protest, food is presented as an abject object. Each prison meal, served on a garish blue plastic plate, consists of a portion of greyish matter accompanied by two slices of white bread and topped with a lump of butter. In one scene, McCann looks down at his plate with disgust before flinging it against a wall smeared in excrement. Kristeva describes the conditions in which food becomes an abject object. She writes,

> When food appears as a polluting object, it does so as oral object only to the extent that orality signifies a boundary of the self's clean and proper body. Food becomes abject only if it is a border between two distinct entities or territories. A boundary between nature and culture, between the human and the non-human.[34]

In throwing the meal against a wall coated in excrement, food's potential as a polluting agent is illustrated. By framing food in this manner, the boundary between nature and culture is fractured. The prisoners taking part in the dirty protest capitalize on the boundary position of food by using its end product as a powerful if primitive weapon to debase the culture of the prison system.

32 Sands, *One day*, p. 51.   33 Cardinal Ó Fiaich reporting his visit to the H-Blocks in 1978, viewed at http://www.bobbysandstrust.org/blanket.asp 29/04/05.   34 Kristeva, *Powers of horror*, p. 75.

The Hunger Strikers also use food, by converting their suffering from its deprivation into a means to disturb that same culture.

THE SACRIFICIAL AESTHETIC

Religious settings strengthen *H3*'s sacrificial theme: Scullion discusses the option of going on hunger strike in a scene in which a priest is saying mass. Furthermore, religious imagery infuses the entire film: the prison cells are bathed in a white light while the prisoners' long hair and makeshift clothing lend them a resemblance to Christ's apostles. Their allegiance to Sands can be interpreted as a form of devotion, since it is owing to his endorsement of the Hunger Strikes that the others participate. Although the prisoners have been convicted for paramilitary activities, the film narrative omits any mention of prisoners' activities prior to their convictions – apart from a brief flashback experienced by McCann that recalls an ambush along a country road leading to his capture by the RUC. By carefully emphasizing the suffering of members of the republican movement rather than their engagement in criminal activities, *H3* promotes a distinction between pure and impure violence as elucidated in another context by Girard.[35] Through its aesthetic and narrative mode of address, the film construes the prisoners' self-directed violence as being 'pure' or legitimate political violence as opposed to 'impure' or illegitimate sectarian violence.

In historical terms, public consciousness of the act of self-sacrifice was magnified after the events of the 1916 Rising, which were strategically planned by its leader Padraig Pearse to coincide with the Catholic Church's 'Holy Week'. Sweeney describes the political repercussions of the Rising: 'The events of the Easter Rising proved to be a watershed for Anglo-Irish politics and for the tradition of militant republicanism. The Rising, coinciding with the Catholic Church's 'Holy Week' and the honouring of the resurrection of Christ, has been described as 'a bloody protest'.[36] Similar to the Maze hunger strikers, the 1916 rebels pitted themselves against the might of the British state despite overwhelming odds against their success. Despite *H3*'s brief allusion to at least one prisoner's engagement in paramilitary activities prior to his capture, the narrative emphasizes the prisoners' struggle inside the prison to achieve self-determination and to distinguish themselves from ordinary criminals. As previously stated, the violence they inflict upon their own bodies through self-starvation is presented in terms of pure or sacrificial violence, and as such unifies religious and political themes. Pearse extolled the virtues of dying for one's nation in a famous speech in which he declared: 'Life springs from death; and from

---

35 René Girard, *Violence and the sacred* (London, 1988), p. 39.   36 Sweeney, 'Irish Hunger Strikes', p. 425.

the graves of patriot men and women spring living nations'.[37] The execution
of the twelve signatories of the 1916 proclamation of independence led to their
martyrdom and their deaths were perceived as sacrifices on behalf of the nation.
One prisoner's exclamation of the republican catch cry 'Tiocfaidh ar lá', or
'Our day will come', situates *H3*'s address within this larger, nationalist narrative in which self-sacrifice emerges as a recurrent theme.

POLICING CRISIS

Girard observes that sacrifice languishes in societies that have a firmly established judicial system.[38] This might explain why historically hunger strikes
have been such effective strategies in those places where the judiciary has not
been beyond reproach. Inspired by the H-Block strikes, young political prisoners on South Africa's Robben Island,[39] including Nelson Mandela, went on
hunger strike and succeeded in their aims.[40] While Northern Ireland has not
been without a judicial system, there has been disapproval of police forces in
that jurisdiction since the foundation of the partitionist state. The predominantly Protestant make-up of these forces has attracted ample criticism.
Additionally, general mistrust on the part of the nationalist community of the
British legal establishment proved justified when the wrongful imprisonment
of the Guildford Four and the Birmingham Six was acknowledged. Such a
historical context suggests why the hunger strikes were interpreted unilater-
ally by Republicans as sacrifices on behalf of the nationalist community. Girard
also notes how sacrifice surfaces when there is a threat to the collective existence of a group. *H3* identifies the threat posed by the criminalization of political prisoners to the identity of the larger nationalist community who refused
to recognize the legitimacy of the Northern Irish state in the early 1980s, while
simultaneously keying into contemporary concerns over the status of the republican movement. Girard writes,

> In societies that practice sacrifice there is no critical situation to which
> the rites are applicable, but there are certain crises that seem to be
> particularly amenable to sacrificial mediation. In these crises the social
> fabric of the community is threatened; dissension and discord are rife.

37 A subsection of an internet site entitled *Pearse, Patrick (1879–1916)* viewed at http://www.
giveirelandbacktotheirish.com/pearse.htm 21/03/05. 38 Girard, *Violence*, p. 18. 39 Those
who lived on Robben Island included the mentally ill, lepers and prisoners. Their geographic
isolation was intended to exclude them from the rest of society. The dehumanizing treatment
endured by prisoners on the island has been well documented. On Mandela's arrival, the wardens
shouted, 'this is the island. Here you will die like animals'. Viewed at: http://www.
robben-island.org.za/departments/heritage/gallery/mandela.asp , 23/03/05 40 Denis O'Hearn,
'The limits of memory', *Village*, 12–18 March 2005.

The more critical the situation, the more 'precious' the sacrificial victim must be.[41]

In *H3*, the prisoners' euphoric response to the news of Sands' election to parliament highlights his status as a 'precious victim' and marks his anticipated death as emphatically symbolic. *H3*'s aesthetic mould evokes the religious connotations of self-sacrifice to buttress the political function of Sands' death. Visited by Scullion on his deathbed, Sands bears an uncanny resemblance to the image of Jesus Christ. By sacrificing their lives, the prisoners are shown attempting to reconcile the contradiction between their religious duties and commitment to political violence in order to capitalize on the beneficent properties of sacrificial violence.[42] On visual evidence alone, the prisoners could pass for a cast playing the apostles in a biblical drama. Through an aesthetic design suffused with religious imagery, *H3* constructs the prisoners struggle as a 'saintly', if contradictory, one.

Girard uses the term 'sacrificial crisis' to describe the disappearance of the difference between impure and purifying violence. In this event, purification is no longer possible and reciprocal violence spreads throughout the community.[43] *H3* revisits a period that has since been succeeded by such a crisis. Arguably, the hunger strikes occurred at a time in republican history when militant republicans could still present their actions within the framework of sacrifice or purifying violence. Recent developments, such as the Northern Irish bank robbery and the killing of John McCartney, as well as activities such as money laundering, fuel smuggling, loan sharking and extortion[44] have confirmed, beyond rebuke, that criminality has become an integral component of the republican movement. Such instances demonstrate a breakdown in the ritualistic nature of sacrifice elucidated by Girard, which is designed to 'keep violence *outside* the community'.[45] The republican movement's inability to convey convincingly their separation from criminal violence resembles Girard's description of the sacrificial crisis:

> The sacrificial crisis can be defined, therefore, as a crisis of distinctions – that is, a crisis affecting the cultural order. This cultural order is nothing more than a regulated system of distinctions in which the differences among individuals are used to establish their "identity" and their mutual relationships.[46]

41 Girard, *Violence*, p. 18.   42 Ibid., p. 37.   43 Ibid., p. 49.   44 An article entitled 'Criminal activities of the IRA are not going away' in the *Irish Times* 05/09/05 describes the weekly losses to the Revenue as a result of IRA activity. Accessed on-line at: http://www.ireland.com/newspaper/ireland/2005/0905/2760800352AG05LALLY.html on 13/09/05.   45 Girard, *Violence*, p. 92.   46 Ibid., p. 49.

It is ironic that *H3* remembers the prisoners' resistance to criminalization during a period when the criminality of that movement is so prominent. Despite this, the peace process has enabled the re-signification of the dirty protest and hunger strikes to occur at the level of popular representation. The term 'peripheral memorial' can be employed to specify how *H3* commemorates the losses and suffering of those in the H-Blocks in sacrificial terms. Its narrative address is strengthened through analogies to Christian suffering and the screenplay anchors prisoners' suffering within a nationalist and republican tradition by echoing those discourses. *H3* proposes that the prisoners participated in abject behaviour in order to destabilize a symbolic system that threatened their identity as political prisoners through legislation and dehumanizing treatment. While the Hunger Strikes were not a customary subject in popular representation, in reality, they marked a turning point in the history of the troubles. They are now considered responsible for a massive upsurge in support for the Sinn Fein party, and as a key reason for the British government signing the Anglo Irish Agreement in 1985.[47] *H3* commemorates the self-abjection and self-sacrifice of the H-Block prisoners in an audio-visual culture that has overcome much of the timidity evident in earlier explorations of the past.

---

47 This is argued in 'Cain Web Service: The Hunger Strike of 1981 – Summary', viewed at http://cain.ulst.ac.uk/events/hstrike/summary.htm 16/02/05.

Sectarian violence in contemporary Indian cinema: aesthetics of *Dev* (2004) and *Mr and Mrs Iyer* (2002)

RASHMI SAWHNEY

In February-March 2002, India witnessed one of the most horrific and systematic assaults on the Muslim community in Gujarat. This shameful event in Indian history followed previous episodic bursts of violence seen in 1984 in the riots against the Sikh community, in 1993 during the Bombay blasts, and in the aftermath of the demolition of the Babri Masjid in 1992. These recent incidences of sectarian violence are the consequence of a twelve-hundred-year-long history of the Indian subcontinent, which has led to the creation of a complex relationship of exchange and conflict between Hindu, Muslim, and Christian communities in India.[1] In the nineteenth and twentieth centuries, colonial rule and the ensuing freedom struggle assigned central importance to the question of 'identity', of distinguishing the self from the other. In fiction and popular culture, the image of the other crystallized after passing through the filters of history, memory and myth.

Needless to say, in a multi-religious country like India, the Hindu–Muslim–Sikh–Christian relationship has been of central concern to the Indian state and has led to various endeavours to produce and circulate popular imagery to sustain the sanctity of a socially integrated nation.[2] The enterprise of the Indian state in dealing at a socio-political level with various separatist movements based on language, creed and caste,[3] has come to be an essential

---

1 The term 'Hindu' was not in vogue in India until about the beginning of the second millennium. It came in as an external identification of people living along the banks of the Sindhu River who used to follow various heterodox worship practices. Islam arrived in India a little before the beginning of the second millennium. Christianity in India has a twin origin: first, the Syrian Christians in Kerala accepted the teachings of Jesus in the first century from one of the direct followers of Christ who landed on the southern coast of India, and then the Catholic Church had its impact through the Portuguese colonization of Goa during the fifteenth century. The Sikh faith emerged during the sixteenth century and stabilized itself in the north-western region of the five rivers, the Punjab. All these religions have coexisted in India, necessarily involving a complex history of collaboration and conflict. **2** The most undisguised examples of these are the Door Darshan telecast short promotional films on national integration such as *Mile Sur Mera Tumhara* ('Let Our Timbres Meet', 1988) or *Ek Titli, Anek Titeliya* (One Butterfly, Many Butterflies, 1984), which attempt to represent the entire nation as a unified entity. **3** These have included the

component of Indian film narratives. These concern themselves with defining and generating, what Sunil Khilnani[4] calls 'the idea of India'. Just like the Indian state, in order to imagine the nation, Indian cinema has perforce needed to imagine its 'other'. This image is drawn by the Indian cinema partly from state-sponsored ideas, and partly from a collective reservoir of people's cultural consciousness and memory. Yet, at all times, the image of the other has been a reflection of larger trends in national and world politics and the Indian state's ideological stance in relation to these in the international arena. In the early years of independence the most common sign system to define the self and the other was based on the East/West, traditional/modern binary, a project which could be seen as the residue of the nationalist movement of the nineteenth and twentieth centuries. In early post-independence India, when an openly socialist and liberal humanist approach to development was adopted by the Nehru government, the city-bred bourgeoisie, the rich industrialist and the feudal oppressor were all categorized as enemies of the nation in cinema. The representation of the other/outsider/enemy in cinema is material for a separate essay, but for the purpose of this paper, I will point out that the imagined other in cinema, represents a potential threat to the camaraderie amongst the multi-religious yet 'Indianized' communities that make up the fabric of the imaginary unified national entity in Indian films.

Dev (Govind Nihalani, 2004) and *Mr and Mrs Iyer* (Aparna Sen, 2002) are significant milestones in Indian cinema. Both films take up the question of the (national) self and the other in the context of the less frequently addressed issue of sectarian violence in Indian cinema. More importantly, both films generate modes of address which attempt to evaluate the position of the *majority* (Hindu) community as passive supporters of politically instigated religious intolerance in the country. These two films are indicative of the extent of the crisis threatening secularism in India, which is conveyed through the depiction of widespread religious misconceptions, the failure of state governance to maintain secular credentials, and the misuse of religion for political purposes.

In interviews with the media, Govind Nihalani has voiced concern over the politicization and communalization of governing and law-enforcing bodies in the country, and states that his objective in *Dev* was to highlight this issue.[5]

Liberation Tigers of Tamil Elam's (LTTE) demands in Southern India, separatist movements in the North-Eastern states, the Akali Dal's one-time demand for a separate Punjab, or the Indian government's recognition of Jharkhand as a separate state in recent years. Indian cinema has usually viewed such issues from a nationalistic perspective, as seen for example in Mani Ratnam's *Dil Se* (1998), and, less commonly, from a humanist perspective, as in Santosh Sivan's *Terrorist* (1998). 4 Sunil Khilnani, *The idea of India* (Delhi, 2003). 5 '*Dev* deals with current politics. It explores the efforts to politicize and communalize various institutions and the police force. It raises questions on the relationship between authority and constitutionality. The scourge of communalism is seen through the perspective of the police.' As stated in 'A film must appeal to people'. Interview with Saibal Chatterjee (2004) in *HindustanTimes.com Special* available at

Aparna Sen's intention in *Mr and Mrs Iyer*, on the other hand, was to use sectarian violence as a backdrop to the story of a journey. Sen's description of *Mr and Mrs Iyer* as a 'road film' can be misleading about the critical comment the film has to offer on religious intolerance in wider society. In interviews with the media, Sen has strongly expressed her alarm over the rise of fundamentalism in India, and this concern comes through in many ways in *Mr and Mrs Iyer*.[6] A critical factor that must be taken into account while analyzing the two films is that they were punctuated by the bloody Gujarat riots of 2002 and this invests each of them with a different urgency of persuasion. *Dev* is a fictionalized presentation inspired by the Gujarat riots with a plot that is reminiscent of the aftermath of the train-burning incident at Godhra.[7] The making of *Mr and Mrs Iyer* was preceded by the attack on the Indian parliament on 13 December 2001. In this essay I take the view that both films employ cinematic techniques and devices with the purpose of implicating the spectator as a passive, yet accountable, accomplice of the violence, thereby creating an active dynamic between narrative, image and spectator.

While *Dev* and *Mr and Mrs Iyer* may be seen together as films that share a common concern, their intended spectator, and therefore their styles and aesthetics, are distinctly different. *Dev*, a Hindi film, made within the modes of conventional popular Hindi cinema (with a romantic angle, song and music, star cast, and a length of three hours) is aimed at the masses.[8] *Mr and Mrs Iyer* does not last the full three hours and its use of the English language, restricts its viewership to a primarily urban upper- and middle-class audience.[9] While *Dev* attempts to wrestle with fairly multifarious notions, and is composed of fast-paced editing and protracted dialogues, *Mr and Mrs Iyer* has a more straightforward plot and follows a slow meditative rhythm, concerning

http://www.hindustantimes.com/govindnihalani/interview.shtml.   6 'I have been deeply concerned about the ugly head of fundamentalism that has been ravaging the country continuously. Violence once had no place in Indian society or its thought process. I have expressed this concern time and again in my editorials in *Sananda*, the Kolkata woman's fortnightly that I edit. It pains me to see that the secularism that Jawaharlal Nehru and Mahatma Gandhi stood up for is almost extinct. Even among the urban middle class and the upper middle class, the so-called educated, enlightened class, secularism is absent.' Quoted in 'Aparna Sen makes a statement again', Interview with Deepali Nandwani (July 2002) in *Rediffmovies* available at http://www. rediff.com/entertai/2002/jul/27aparna.htm.   7 It includes elements that bear resemblance to the Best Bakery case, the alleged involvement of the chief minister and government officials in delaying police reinforcements to curb the violence, the coming forward of a lone girl as witness, and the organized assaults against the Muslim community that resulted in widespread displacement, destruction and death.   8 'Where a film comes from is determined by the creator's sensibility and convictions, but for any film to be really effective, it should appeal to people. I am fully aware that if a film does not recover its cost it would be difficult for a director to make his next film.' Quoted in 'Aparna Sen makes a statement again'.   9 'English is the medium of communication for people all over India. I am also trying to reach the urban, young, English-speaking audience both in India and abroad.' Quoted in 'A film must appeal to people'.

itself with a world that is for the most part, English speaking, urban, middle class, multi-cultural and cosmopolitan.

Both films draw on the conventions of realism. That Sen and Nihalani should choose a realist aesthetic will come as no surprise to readers who are familiar with their films. Nihalani's career began as a cinematographer in 1962 with Satyadev Dubey's *Shantata! Court Chalu Aahe*, and he had an especially rewarding association with Shyam Benegal for whom he filmed several documentaries and ten feature films. Almost two decades later, in 1981, he directed *Akrosh*, the first of his twelve directorial ventures for television and cinema. Nihalani's left-oriented ideology is evident from his aesthetic approach towards direction and cinematography, as well as his choice of subjects. Several of his films have been adaptations of radical literary texts including Mahasweta Devi's *Hazar Chaurasi ki Ma* (Mother of 1084), Strindberg's *The Father*, Federico Garcia Lorca's *The House of Bernarda Alba*, and Bhisham Shahni's *Tamas*.

Aparna Sen is amongst India's best-known women directors, who began as an actress in Bengali films, and in 1981, the same year that Nihalani began his directorial career, made her mark as a director with *36 Chowringhee Lane*. Sen has directed seven feature films with her latest, *15 Park Avenue*, released for public viewing in January 2006. The two most significant influences on Sen's approach to cinema have been Chidananda Das Gupta, her father, an eminent filmmaker and critic, and Satyajit Ray, Sen's first director and her father's close associate in founding the Calcutta Film Society. The liberal-humanist approach that Sen inherited from her father and from Satyajit Ray leaves an indelible mark on her cinema; her films respect modernist aesthetics but retain a strong link with social issues.

It is worthwhile to recollect Colin MacCabe's seminal essay on realism to put the two films considered here in proper context. MacCabe extends his observations of the nineteenth-century novel to cinematic realism and argues that the hierarchy of truth established by rendering the metalanguage transparent in the literary form occurs in cinema by the position of privilege accorded to the narrative prose. 'The camera shows us what happens – it tells us the truth against which we can measure the discourses'.[10] A classic realist film, by MacCabe's argument, can sustain no contradiction between the visual and verbal components of a film or, if it does, then the visual component of the film establishes the superior truth and reality for the spectator. MacCabe also points out that a film is classified as realist not on the basis of its thematic subject, but on the basis of the manner in which the narrative is ordered.

In *Dev*, the narrative is ordered as a relay between discourse (through dialogue) and visual images. Both elements work together, as well as in opposition, to establish the truth of the narrative. But the demands of rationality that realism makes on the narrative collapses midway through the film. The hier-

10 Colin MacCabe, *Theoretical essays: film, linguistics, literature* (London, 1985).

archical ordering between the visual and verbal elements of cinema is in fact used to facilitate this momentary break from realism. In *Mr and Mrs Iyer*, the illusion of realism is thrown into doubt through the self-conscious use of a camera lens as the visible apparatus enabling vision for the characters of the film. As a consequence, the rational resolution of the problem that might be attempted through realism, shifts location to what I suggest is a metaphysical level in *Mr and Mrs Iyer*, and a divine iconic command in *Dev*. While the films allow conflicting visions to articulate themselves through various discourses, the final resolution of conflict between self and other occurs by privileging a particular point of view, which in the case of these two films, is that of a secular nation.

NARRATIVE STRUCTURE AND THE HIERARCHY OF TRUTH IN 'DEV'

In *Dev* the contradiction between state/individual, Hindu/Muslim, and secular/fundamental is brought to life through a formal construction that suggests resemblance to the idea of stasis. Stasis means 'standstill' or 'conflict,' and in rhetorical terms indicates the 'point in an argument that must be resolved for a discussion to come to a conclusion'.[11] The theory of stasis was first compiled by Hermagoras,[12] and he defines it as consisting of four stages, each of which propels the dialogue in a forward direction, defining its scope and eliminating excess, in order to reach the final point of resolution. Each stage of the stasis serves a specific purpose to enable debate and discussion in an orderly and fruitful manner. The cinematic rhetoric of *Dev*, and thereby its ability to involve directly the viewer in the narrative, is structured on the pattern of a stasis sequence. However, the assembly of sequences involves a failure in logical resolution that results in a break from realist conventions towards the end of the film.

Each unit of the stasis sequence contains and expounds the debate through a combination of rational dialogue and an emotive visual component. The dialogue sequences take on an iconic[13] dimension through their staging and are juxtaposed with the emotive components of the sequence. The pivotal incident that inspires the emotive components is the death of Dev and Bharati's

---

11 William Covino and David Jollife, *Rhetoric* (Boston, 1995).   12 Hermagoras of Temnos was a first century BC Greek philosopher who achieved great reputation as a rhetorician of the Rhodian school. He was a teacher of oratory in Rome, and is considered to have invented the doctrine of *stasis*. The theory of *stasis* has continued to influence contemporary study of rhetoric, and is considered to hold place amongst its classical tenets.   13 I use the term 'iconic' here not in the sense it has been used by Rajadhyaksha to describe Phalke's and early silent Indian mythological films' attempt to combine traditional representational elements with a modern perspective through frontal cinematic images that he describes as iconic, but in the sense that the term is referred to in structuralist philosophy as 'standing in for' or allegorizing something else.

Table 1.1 Stasis Sequence

Stasis sequence and purpose	*Question asked*	*Cultural context*
I. *Stochasmos* Defines undisputed facts in a given situation which underline the argument, and form the mutual understanding between parties	Philosophy of action and inaction, or the individual's duty towards the nation/society. Both Dev and Tej are commonly agreed upon the fact that action is an important duty of the individual.	1. The *Bhagavada Gita*, Krishna's treatise on action/inaction to Arjun in the Mahabharata war. 2. Politicization of the Krishna figure by right-wing parties such as the Vishwa Hindu Parishad and the Bharatiya Janta Party.
II. *Horos* Defines key terms of the situation. By resolving disputes on key terms, the stasis becomes much clearer because this helps to bring the audience closer to the intentions of the actors.	The action plan or what must be done with the enemy.	1. Political ideologies are clarified by invoking Adolf Hitler, Lokmanya Tilak, Veer Savarkar, Mahatma Gandhi and Jawaharlal Nehru. 2. Reference to the term 'pseudosecularism'[14] positions Tej clearly as a Hindu nationalist. 3. Reference to Dev as suitable for role of 'member of opposition' historically situates the narrative during BJP rule, and aligns Dev with the Congress ideology.
III. *Poiotes* Limits the argument, condensing it to the necessary and pertinent information.	The question is limited to individual action paths, based on each protagonist's idea of right and wrong.	1. Again draws from the Gita's philosophy of action/inaction. 2. The open frame situates the dialogue within a wider social context (not limited merely to discussions between the two officers).
IV *Metalepsis* The resolution of the stasis, the point of it all, is explicitly made clear to the viewer.	What is the point of it all, i.e. the point of the spectator's viewing of the film. This question is posed in relation to the spectator's role as citizen of the nation.	1. Drawing from the mythological film tradition, proscenium theatre and painting, the frontal iconic confrontation of the image resonates of a divine injunction. 2. Amitabh Bachchan's God-like status in Indian society is invoked to instruct the spectator.

14 The term 'pseudo-secularism' was first used by L.K. Advani, senior leader of the Bharatiya Janta Party, to describe secular politics in the country, which in his opinion (and that of the party) gives in to unwarranted minority demands.

Mise-en-scène	*Answers generated*	*Resolved and unresolved elements*
The scene is shot in Dev's dinning room; cinematic frame includes dining table with bottles of alcohol, painting, photo of Armaan, lampshades; Dev and Tej stand near dining table, Bharati sits on sofa (symbolizing exclusion from conversation); shot-reverse-shot editing; sequence ends with descriptive verbal recounting of Armaan's death.	Each actor puts forward their own interpretation of the *Gita*. Dev's philosophy of action is based on upholding constitutional values, and a vision of an economically progressive nation. Tej's is based on physical strength and force. Bharati doesn't believe in the Gita, but she desires an egalitarian, just, and respectful society.	Agreed upon – 1. Action must be taken. 2. Action must be directed towards the enemy (to guard the nation). In Question – The identity of the enemy.
Similar staging as of sequence I; the scene is shot in Tej's dining room; extensive use of shot-reverse-shot to highlight actors' emotions; sequence is cut by a shot of Farhaan lying prostrate and unconscious on the prison cell floor, and the next shot of Aaliya, head draped in a veil, praying for Frahaan's life; sequence ends with a graphic b/w flashback of Armaan's death.	The identity of the enemy is implicated in the action plan. Tej is clear that the enemy is the Indian Muslim, shown formally through a sound-image overlap. Dev is clear that the enemy are forces instigating communal hatred and violence.	1. Ideological context and stance of each actor is made clear. 2. Father-son relationship between Dev and Armaan/Farhaan is established for the spectator. 3. The identity of the enemy still remains contested by the two actors. After this sequence any possibility of resolution of conflict is lost, as the Muslim colony is burnt and looted, the police force is prevented from helping on orders from the CM, and Dev resigns from his job.
Open frame, breaks from iconic convention of earlier sequences; both characters captured within a single frame; shot-reverse-shot not used and this highlights the detached nature of the dialogue and broken relationship between the men; they overlook a parapet by the sea, early evening sun; exit route taken by Tej marked by a wooden door symbolizing the occupation of two different worlds by the two men.	The stasis has reached breaking point now. The dialogue cannot move forward through speech, only through action. Therefore, both men are now pursuing their individual paths – Dev has filed a case to defend the Muslim victims, and Tej attempts to kill Dev in a later scene.	The ideological positions have been established clearly for/by the spectator; the secular point of view is now depicted as the superior one – the formal and literal dialogue between the two viewpoints has ceased. Following this scene, Dev is killed, and Tej commits suicide. Thus, the rational progression of the dialogue ends with the death of the protagonists.
A close up of the actor, confronting the viewer by directly looking into the camera lens; camera zooms in very slowly to show an extreme close up shot.	The viewer is told that the point of central importance is the continuing process of struggle and the fight against injustice – not that of victory/ defeat or life/death.	The importance of individual (spectator's) action is foregrounded. The rational dialogue between secularism/fundamentalism generates a number of spectatorial positions; all of these are in the end collapsed into a single dominant position which is established outside the rational dialogue, through melodramatic and emotive elements of the plot (e.g. Farhaan's substitution of the lost son, Aaliya's honesty in the face of violent politics, Dev's murder by Tej, Tej's own guilt and his suicide)

son Armaan, who has been shot by Muslim militants. The lost son takes on a symbolic value, signifying the personal loss endured to create a future state which embodies an egalitarian society, representative of the liberal secular and economically progressive nation envisaged by Jawaharlal Nehru. At a later stage in the narrative, the emptiness that has been created by the son's death is filled by the discovery of Farhaan, a Muslim boy, who claims inheritance of the secular state as imagined by Dev. The rationalization of the ideologies is supplemented by an appeal to the unconscious beckoning of blood, the universal cause of violence; blood which is lost through the dead son and regained through his rediscovery as the Muslim youth.

There are four such sequential units involving two police officers, Dev and Tej, and each of these constitutes one part of the stasis that leads to an answer to the primary question – the question of the responsibility of the viewer (who is assumed to be Hindu in the mode of address of the film) towards protecting the Indian constitution and its secular vision. A description of individual units of stasis, development of its four stages, and the break in narrative logic is represented in tabular form here which allows descriptive details of individual stasis units to be considered in context of the larger structural linkages and differences between units. Each stage of stasis is analyzed using six parameters which evaluate the objective of the stasis-stage, the dynamic of dialogue and visuals to generate questions and responses in order to fulfill the objective, the cinematic staging of the sequence, and the cultural context of the issues generated. The table given below represents each stasis sequence in three dimensions: rational (as developed through language), cultural (by providing a socio-historical context), and formal (as suggested through staging and through theatrical and cinematic conventions of visual representation). The stasis sequence is described in detail in the table and is briefly summarized subsequently.

The four stages of stasis as defined by Hermagoras and discussed in the table above are *stochasmos, horos, poites,* and *metalepsis,* leading finally to the resolution of the issue. The first stage, *stochasmos,* defines undisputed facts in a given situation which underline the argument, and form the mutual understanding between parties. The first sequence of the stasis takes up the question of philosophizing action and inaction, or the individual's duty towards the nation and society. Both men start with the commonly accepted premise that 'action' is an important part of their duties drawing on the philosophy of the *Bhagvada Gita.*[15]

Horos, the second stage of stasis defines key terms to the situation and it is in this sequence that it is determined that action must be taken against an 'enemy'. However, the identity of the enemy is contentious, and this debate

15 The verses of the *Bhagavada Gita* are Krishna's instructions to Arjun on the philosophy of action and inaction, narrated in the context of the Mahabharata war.

is enacted in the second stasis stage. The entry point into this sequence is a sound-image overlap, where a mid-shot of Farhaan being interrogated is superimposed with Tej's voice condemning him as a terrorist. Farhaan's image enables the transition into the second discussion and is the associative link between the first and second stages of the stasis sequence. This scene is cut by two shots that create the diegesis for the secular argument: a high angle pan shot from the shadows of the cell bars to an unconscious Farhaan lying prostrate on the prison cell floor resembling a hunted and trapped animal, and a shot of Aaliya on bent knees with head draped in a white veil, praying for Farhaan's life. Both shots are cryptic images of despair and subjection, and highlight the inhumanity of the intellectualized conversation between Tej and Dev that follows. The sequence ends with a black and white flashback recounting Armaan's death at the hands of Muslim militants, substantiating Tej's fundamentalist arguments with emotional visual impact. In this sequence the dialogues underscore the ideological tension, attempting serious engagement with the issue of communalism. The visual component, on the other hand, functions in an associative manner, establishing Farhaan as Dev's symbolic son, and generating a meta-narrative which invests the secular viewpoint with a dominant truth value. The divergent narratives of the two components of the film – dialogue and image – indicate the impossibility of resolution, and suggest that the final solution will be driven by the image, which in the case of *Dev* assumes an iconic form, as indicated in the table.

The stasis and dynamic tension emanates from the perception of the state as a debilitated entity, lacking all will to control the destinies of the citizens in tune with its professed egalitarian and secular mission. After the second stage the stasis begins to break away from its development to a logical resolution and a flurry of events in the film lead to the destruction of any possibility of existence of the secular ideal. The Muslim colony is attacked by politically instigated riots, shops are destroyed, women raped, people killed and burned alive. In the face of this violence, the state and its apparatus – the police as well as parliamentary bureaucracy – are unable, or unwilling, to prevent the destruction caused. Dev's desperate attempts to help the riot victims find justice result in his own destruction, first symbolically, and then literally. The third stage of stasis represents the break from logical resolution through both formal and discursive methods. The end of a rational resolution towards the ideal of a secular nation is represented by the director through blackout editing between a shot of a defeated Dev crying with his head in his hands, and the next shot of Dev handing in his resignation to the Chief Minister. The inability to bridge the gap between the two ideological positions results in first, the death of Dev, who is shot by a bullet from Tej's revolver, and later Tej's own suicide. Therefore, the stage is set to address the real question (of the citizen-viewer's role) only after both the 'onlookers' and power-wielders have been annihilated.

Why does the narrative seek escape from the demands of rationality and linearity imposed by realism? The tentative answer I volunteer here requires a brief return to Laura Mulvey's ground-breaking 1975 essay.[16] Mulvey identifies three kinds of looks in narrative cinema – the first look is that of the camera recording the pro-filmic event; the second look is of the audience watching the final product; and the third look is of the characters looking at each other within the screen illusion. Mulvey argues that narrative cinema subordinates the first two looks to the third, eliminates intrusive camera presence and prevents a distancing awareness in the audience. Developing Mulvey's argument in a different context, Ashish Rajadhyaksha has pointed out that in realist cinema, the camera's vision of pro-filmic reality must be concurrent with the spectator's gaze at the film, or that the first and second look are the same. This implies that the mode of address used in each film ought to correspond with the subjectivity of the spectator as envisaged by the makers of the film.[17]

While dealing with an issue that has social or political bearing, realist cinema demands a degree of detached objectivity, which becomes possible only when the subject is the 'other'. *Dev* encounters difficulties at two levels. Firstly, the objectivity required becomes difficult to fulfil because the point of view of the narrator is that of a middle-class police officer, a person in a position of power, who acts as a guardian of the marginalized viewpoint. Therefore, the film directs the camera to turn upon the spectator (presumed to be Hindu in the mode of address of *Dev*), a tactic which usually requires an element of satire or distance and difficult to achieve through realism. The second reason may be that internalization of aggression, extreme bodily discipline and control, and searching for solutions within the 'self', have been characteristics of the Indian civilization in many ways, and therefore, the approach of introspection adopted in *Dev* represents not only the criticality of social circumstances, but perhaps is already a familiar solution to Hindus. This is executed through frontal confrontation of the spectator, where the second and third looks intersect, and is a visual format that enjoys a long history of representation ranging from painting to proscenium theatre in the country.[18]

LOOKING INWARDS THROUGH THE EYE OF THE CAMERA

In contrast to *Dev*, *Mr and Mrs Iyer* brings to life the violence entailed in the threat to secularism and in narrow-minded, caste-based prejudices through

16 Laura Mulvey, 'Visual pleasure and narrative cinema', *Screen*, 16:3 (1975), pp 6–18.   17 Ashish Rajadhyaksha, 'Viewership and Democracy in the Cinema' in R. Vasudevan (ed.), *Making meaning in Indian cinema* (New Delhi, 2001).   18 Madhava Prasad's discussion of *darsana* in 'The absolutist gaze: political structure and cultural form' provides very good insights on this subject. Madhava Prasad, *Ideology of the Hindi film: a historical construction* (Delhi, 1998)

the opposite of a stasis, by weaving its plot around an actual and metaphorical journey. One of the primary differences between the two films, is that *Dev* implicates the viewer in the ideological conflict from the point of view of the power wielders while *Mr and Mrs Iyer* recreats the conflict outside the parameters of the state, situating it amidst the common people, and therefore the viewers themselves. The journey on the 'little red bus' from the hills of Himachal to the plains of Calcutta stages the transgression of religious identities through a metaphorical journey undertaken by the female protagonist, by way of which, the film destabilizes religion-based stereotypes and generates a secular viewing-position.

The film begins with a fairy-tale like narrative voice that belongs to a respectable, educated, middle aged man, suggestive of Chacha Nehru[19] narrating a children's story. The voice of the narrator clearly spells out the cultural context of the narrative as belonging to a multi-lingual, multi-cultural, and secular India. The ideological stance of the film is made clear at the outset and the secular point of view is privileged from the very beginning. The narrative is organized into three segments, the first representing a physical journey, the second an imaginary journey, and the third, both real and imaginary journeys undertaken together by the two protagonists, Meenakshi Iyer, a Tamil Brahmin wife and mother, and Jahangir Chowdhury (Raja), a Muslim wildlife photographer. The passengers on the bus are caught in religious rioting and an ensuing curfew, whereby Raja and Meenakshi are forced to spend time together and begin to identify with each other's worlds. Raja literally dons the identity of a Tamil Brahmin, when Meenakshi introduces him as 'Mr Iyer' to the Hindu mobs who throng the bus with the intention of killing any Muslims on board. Meenakshi gradually begins to imagine herself as Raja's partner and in one instance also as a Muslim woman, when she looks at her face in the mirror without the *bindi*, the sign of a married Hindu woman. The exchange of identities is symbolized through the transfer of fluid, of shared drinking water, an act that invokes rituals of purity and pollution ingrained in Indian society.

The film does not try to generate a rational dialogue between Hindu/Muslim or fundamental/secular viewpoints. In the only scene where Raja initiates a dialogue, recounting the 1984 riots against the Sikh community after the assassination of Indira Gandhi, and the significance of markers of identity in India, his attempts are brushed aside by Meenakshi with the comment 'let's talk of something more pleasant'. It is unclear whether the film tries to actualize the politics of language and silence through gender, or if the silence is a way to escape responsibility on the part of the oppressor.

The scene in the log house encapsulates the essence of the film's rhetoric, where a tableau of the extreme beauty of the wild deer in the moonlit night and

19 Literally meaning 'uncle' Nehru, a term used to refer to Jawaharlal Nehru, which is indicative of his love for children.

the pain of violent murder of a Muslim man are seen and shown through Raja's camera lens. Raja's, and therefore the minority communities', point of view is made visible and comprehensible to Meenakshi, and indeed to the viewer, by enabling a psychological journey into the virtual space inhabited by a Muslim man. Both external reality and internal emotions are mediated through the lens of Raja's camera, making him the controller of the gaze, and of the narrative.

Although Sen uses the realist mode, her realism is quite distinct from the convergence of realism and rationality that can be associated with the early beginnings of the mode under Western industrialization. Sen's realism can be more appropriately described as a metaphysical aesthetic that combines reality and illusion. While the realist mode manoeuvres the narrative, the subjectivity of the spectator is engendered through fantasy and through the excess that is generated in the intersection of the looks of the camera and the spectator. The film invites the majority community to transgress their identities in order to create empathy by holding up an inverted lens to reflect social reality.

The two films, therefore, play around with the conventions of realism in different ways. The element of rhetoric employed in both films introduces an element of persuasion and complicates the objective viewpoint necessary for a realist representation. The spectator is addressed using different conventions and modes in the two films, thereby involving the viewer as citizen/participant in the social situation in different ways. The films engage their viewers through confrontation: *Dev* uses the star persona of Bachchan to instruct the viewer; *Mr and Mrs Iyer* enables the photographic camera to interpret the cinematic narrative from a minority perspective using a journalistic mode. In order to grapple with the challenges of breaking from the demands of realism where the fictionality of the text must be concealed, the spectator's attention is engaged either using familiar visual conventions (such as frontal address) or by enabling identification through the act of transgressive association. The different modes of address in the two films are representative of the intended audience of the films, and the aesthetic approaches employed have potential to implicate the spectator as a contributor to the communal discord and religious intolerance in wider society.

Mirroring narcissism: representation of zainichi in Yukisada Isao's *Go!*

MIKA KO

Yukisada Isao's *Go!* (2001) enjoyed considerable commercial success and won various film awards within Japan. It is a stylish youth drama employing the actor Kubozuka Yôsuke, the top teen heart-throb of Japanese cinema, as its central character. However, one of the main reasons that it attracted critical attention was its theme, that is, the status of Koreans in Japan, or '*zainichi*'. It was the first feature film since Sai Yoichi's *All under the Moon* (1993) to feature zainichi issues and to use a zainichi as a central character.

'Zainichi' is a Japanese word and is one of the most commonly used terms for describing long-term Korean residents in Japan who came, or whose ancestors came, to Japan under Japanese colonialism. Zainichi constitute the largest minority group in Japan and are still treated as second-class citizens in Japanese society. For instance, Japanese citizenship is not given even to the third, fourth or fifth generations without naturalization and zainichi without Japanese citizenship have no vote. To avoid racism, it is not uncommon for zainichi to hide their Korean ethnic background and to pretend to be ethnically Japanese.

Up until the 1990s, representations of zainichi in Japanese cinema had been limited in terms of both quantity and variety. Apart from Nagisa Oshima's *Death by Hanging* in 1968 and a handful of films, mainly of the social drama and the yakuza genres, zainichi were almost invisible in Japanese film or other media. The absence of zainichi and other minority groups in Japanese cinema may not be surprising, given that Japanese official discourse claimed, up until the 1980s, that Japan contained 'no' minorities.[1] In addition, there has been a tendency in the Japanese film industry to avoid, in the form of self-censorship, featuring zainichi or zainichi issues on the grounds that they are either politically too sensitive or too gloomy to be likely to achieve commercial success.

---

1 The first report which Japan submitted in 1980 as a signatory to the United Nations International Covenant on Civil and Political Rights stated that 'minorities do not exist in Japan'. The report was faced with a strong protest from the Ainu (the indigenous people of Hokkaido) and other minority groups in Japan. The second report was submitted in 1987 and this time it stated that, although minorities did exist, there were no minority problem. The then Prime Minister Nakasone also made a notorious remark in 1986, claiming that Japan enjoyed a higher intellectual level because, unlike the United States, it possessed no minorities. See George Hicks, *Japan's hidden apartheid: the Korean minority and the Japanese* (Aldershot, 1997), p. 3.

While the number of films dealing with zainichi has been limited, a certain formula for representing zainichi nevertheless evolved. Zainichi tended to be represented as either the passive victims of social injustice in social drama, or as the source of social problems in yakuza films. These two archetypes, that is, zainichi as either passive victims or the source of social problems, should not be regarded as two opposing images. Rather, the latter may be seen as a variation of the first, since it is often inscribed in the film's narrative that Korean yakuza characters fall into gangsterism as a result of their background, such as racial discrimination, prejudice, and poverty. With a few exceptions, films dealing with zainichi tend to account for the problems of zainichi in terms of Korean ethnicity alone.

Since the 1990s, the commercial success of *All Under the Moon (1993)*, a film directed by a zainichi filmmaker and containing zainichi characters, along with a general trend towards multiculturalism in Japanese society, has led to a significant increase in the number of films (both feature and documentary) dealing with zainichi issues. Isao Yukisada's film *Go!* (2003) is based on a bestselling autobiographical novel written by the young zainichi (or Korean-Japanese as he calls himself) writer, Kazuki Kaneshiro. Like Kaneshiro himself, *Go!*'s main character, Sugihara is a second-generation zainichi who used to have a North Korean nationality, and attended a North Korean-oriented ethnic school, but now has South Korean nationality and attends a Japanese high school. As his voice-over indicates, the narrative consists of 'a love-story' between Sugihara and a Japanese girl and his search for 'identity'.

As David White suggests Yukisada's *Go!*, like the original novel, 'favours commercialism over political content'.[2] While *Go!* contains information about the zainichi's life in Japan that is not well-known (the issue of, for instance, North/South Korean nationalities, the finger-printing of zainichi, the Alien Registration Certificate and so on), the issue of zainichi and their identities is treated in a very superficial fashion reproducing conventional zainichi images. However, in spite of (and maybe because of) such a superficial approach, *Go!* provides a useful text through which to explore issues of identity, subjectivity and the politics of representation. Here, I shall first discuss how zainichi identity/ies is/are represented in the film and then move on to read the film as a text in which various narrational voices and their narcissisms meet and entangle with each other.

Unlike conventional zainichi characters in the past, *Go!*'s main character Sugihara is 'super cool' – a good looking, strong and, at the same time, sensitive young man. The fact that a young Japanese pop idol plays Sugihara's role is in this sense significant, as it effectively creates a 'heart-throb' zainichi

2 David White, 'Zainichi Korean identity in Yukisada Isao's movie *Go!*', a paper presented at the Cultural Typhoon Conference in Okinawa in 2004. I would like to thank David for providing me with a copy of his manuscript.

hero for the first time in Japanese cinema history. Criticising the absence of zainichi characters in Iwai Shunji's *Swallowtail* (1996), Yomota Inuhiko once commented that zainichi were not an 'exotic and ideal object of tourism ... not fashionable when narrating the cosmopolitan atmosphere of contemporary Japan'.[3] However, by using a pop idol as well as flashy visual style, that is often compared with *Trainspotting*, Yukisada's *Go!* makes zainichi fashionable and amenable to consumption.

Despite its ostensible coolness and pop style, however, *Go!*, in fact, does not subvert the conventional representation of zainichi. Sugihara is cool but, like many zainichi characters in Japanese films of the past, he is also a tragic victim of Japanese society in which strong prejudices and discrimination still exist. Nor does the film seem to seek to counter the ideology of Japaneseness as a racially and culturally homogeneous nation. It is evident that the film clearly demarcates its ethnic groups and reproduces the binarism which has traditionally structured the Japanese–Korean divide in terms of both Japanese and zainichi essentialism.

The opening sequence, in this sense, is significant. It starts with Sugihara's voice-over narrating:

> 'Race', 'homeland', 'nation', 'unification', uh, 'patriotism', 'integration', 'compatriot', 'friendship'. They make me sick. 'Rulers', 'repression', 'slaves'? No, 'subjects' is better. 'Aggression', 'discrimination'. What are they? 'Exclusion', 'outcasts', 'blood', 'mixed', 'pure', 'solidarity'.

The camera captures Sugihara's rather brassy face in a close-up shot. Then, after some jump cuts, the camera pulls back to reveal that he is actually in the middle of a basketball match. While his team-mates and opponents rush around with the ball, Sugihara remains standing at the centre of the basketball field. His team-mates and opponents play the game as if Sugihara does not exist. It is not a uni-lateral exclusion of Sugihara by the others, however, as Sugihara himself makes no effort to catch the ball or communicate with his team-mates. He seems vol-untarily to isolate himself. At the end of his voice-over, there is a close-up of a ball in his hands, followed by a tilt of the camera to show Sugihara's face. The next shot is Sugihara from behind, facing his team-mates and opponents. Here Sugihara is separated from the rest by the centre-line. This compositional arrangement clearly presents the demarcation between 'me' and 'them' or 'he' and 'us'. His team-mate approaches him and delivers some blows before moving back again. Sugihara squats down and looks up at the others on the far side of the basketball court. Sugihara's voice-over starts again telling us, 'I was born in Japan.

3 Quoted in Aaron Gerow, 'From the national gaze to multiple gazes: representations of Okinawa in recent Japanese cinema' in Laura Hein and Mark Selden (eds), *Islands of discontent* (New York, 2003).

I am a so-called "Korean-Japanese". I don't think I am any different from the Japanese. But they call me this'. During the narration, the shot/reverse shots, alternately show Sugihara and the rest. The scene assumes a dream or fantasy-like tone in which Sugihara looks perplexed while the reverse shots show the others in soft lighting, dribbling a ball and looking at Sugihara. Responding to Sugihara's voice saying, 'But they call me this', the others shout at Sugihara 'zainichi', throwing their balls towards him. Sugihara then picks up a ball and makes a shoot from an extreme distance. This is followed by Sugihara raging about to the accompaniment of an up-tempo rock soundtrack.

This three-minute sequence sets up Sugihara as a 'strong' 'cool' yet 'victimised' 'hero' fighting Japanese racism alone. It also introduces various issues concerning zainichi and the notion of Japaneseness which excludes zainichi. Sugihara's claim for his identity as a 'Korean–Japanese' is rejected by his Japanese team-mates calling him 'zainichi'. The term 'Korean–Japanese' is not widely accepted in Japanese society, since such a description – connecting two nationalities – potentially upsets the myth of Japanese homogeneity as well as the definition of Japaneseness linked by blood. Although the term 'zainichi' is not necessarily a derogatory word, here it is used (by Sugihara's team-mates) and taken (by Sugihara) to constitute a rejection of Sugihara's Japanese identity and to strait-jacket him within a Korean identity.

Although Sugihara claims a hybrid or 'in-between' identity as 'Korean–Japanese', he is not presented in the film (nor in the original novel) as a character with a hybrid identity. For instance, when he says 'I don't think I am any different from the Japanese', it implies his desire to be the 'same' as other Japanese. In other words, rather than claiming zainichi identity as a form of new hybrid Japanese identity that is characterized by 'difference', or racial and cultural diversity, Sugihara here is trapped in the ideology of 'sameness' or 'homogeneity' involved in defining Japanese identity.

Towards the end of the film, when he sees his girlfriend Sakurai, who rejected him because of his Korean ethnic background, Sugihara criticizes the term 'zainichi' and, by doing so, questions his own identity. When he sees Sakurai waiting for him in the school playground, he asks her, 'Who am I?' Sakurai says nothing. As he keeps repeating the question, she finally says, 'zainichi kankokun-jin' (Korean residents in Japan). As he approaches her, Sugihara shouts:

> How can you call me a zainichi without questioning what it means? By calling me zainichi, it means I am an outsider leaving the country sometime. You understand? I sometime feel I want to kill you fucking Japanese. You are scared. That's why you need to label me. Right? OK, then I am a lion. Lions do not know they are a lion. You fucking gave them that name. Come near me, and I will rip you neck off. Any name is OK, viper, scorpion, or even alien. But I don't think I

am an alien. I am not a zainichi or an alien. I am ME ... I am even
giving up being me. A big question mark. An unknown 'X'. Scared?

Here, Sugihara is questioning the act of 'naming' or 'labelling'. Indeed,
'naming' may be taken to be one of the central themes of *Go!* if we remember
the film starts with a quotation from Shakespeare's *Romeo and Juliet* presented as an inter-title reading:

> What's in a name?
> That which we call a rose
> by any other name would smell as sweet

Thus, Sugihara, at first, seems to be denouncing the act of 'naming' or 'labelling'
as it is the act of controlling or taming. As the French theorist, Maurice Blanchot
has pointed out, naming was a violent act which kept the 'named' at a distance
and at the same time possessed it as a convenient form as a 'name'.[4] For Sugihara
too, being labelled as 'zainichi' means that he is excluded from a Japanese identity but is still under the control of the Japanese who do the defining. However,
to make use of a point made by Judith Butler, what Sugihara overlooks here is
that the name holds out another possibility. Revising Althusser's view of interpellation, Butler argues that 'by being called a name, one is also, paradoxically,
given a certain possibility for social existence, initiated into a temporal life of language that exceeds the prior purposes that animate that call'.[5] Thus, for Butler,
naming has the potential of 'inaugurating a subject in speech who comes to use
language to counter the offensive call'.[6] In the case of zainichi, being called
'zainichi' makes it possible to create a subject position as a zainichi from which
s/he counters or resists the offensive calls and acts. However, this does not happen
in the film and the label 'zainichi' is not invested with any oppositional status.

Moreover, Sugihara's anger is, in fact, directed not towards the act of
naming itself but the gap between the label he wants (Korean–Japanese) and
the one he has been given (zainichi). Sugihara, and the film as a whole, treat
the 'labels' of ethnicity and nationality as exclusive markers for defining and
constructing Sugihara's subjectivity or sense of who he is. After denying the
'zainichi' label, and being denied his 'Korean–Japanese' label, Sugihara claims
that he is giving up being himself and becomes, in his own words, a big 'question mark'. Without the ethnic label, he cannot say who he is.

While the central character Sugihara fails to challenge the ideology of
Japaneseness which defines the Japanese by blood, the possibility of a positive
sense of 'Koreanness' characterized by multiple identities is tentatively implied
through the character Jong-il, Sugihara's best friend from Korean ethnic school.
Jong-il who is rather uncouth yet the brightest student in the school has a

---

4 Maurice Blanchot, *The book to come* trans. Charlotte Mandel (Stanford, 2002).   **5** Judith Butler,
Excited speech: a politics of the performative (New York, 1997), p. 2.   **6** Ibid., p. 2.

Korean father and a Japanese mother. He attends a Korean school at his own wish. Unlike Sugihara, Jong-il neither sees his Koreanness as a burden nor as something of which he should be particularly proud. He is positive about his Koreanness but he is by no means a Korean ethno-nationalist. At one point, Sugihara is hit and denounced by a Korean schoolteacher as 'a traitor to the race' and 'a betrayer of your country' for his decision to transfer to a Japanese school. Sugihara and other students are silent. However, Jong-il stands up and speaks up against the teacher, 'We never had a country'. It is a strong and powerful statement. Unlike Sugihara saying he is rootless, Jong-il does not deny either his Koreanness or Japaneseness, but his statement clearly refuses or criticizes the state authority and educational manipulation which forcibly imposes (North) Korean identity upon him. On a different occasion, Jong-il says that he wants to be a teacher at the Korean school and his dream is to perform a traditional Japanese comedy show with his students at a school festival. His dream may sound trivial. However, in the context of North Korean education within Japan, which does not even allow a student to use any Japanese in school, introducing traditional Japanese performing art at a school event indicates not merely the small dream of an individual but a significant reform.

There is a tendency amongst the zainichi communities in Japan, when criticizing the exclusive nature of Japanese society, to overlook their own essentialist exclusivism. What Jong-il implies in his statement towards the teacher, and contained in his dream, is a refusal of such a narrow sense of Koreanness and his awareness of the need to construct multiple identities or subjectivities. However, towards the end, Jong-il is killed by a Japanese schoolboy. It is not a racist attack. Rather it is based on a tragic misunderstanding. The boy approaches a Korean schoolgirl to confess that he fancies her. The girl is afraid as she thinks that he has approached her to harass her. Jong-il notices her fear and thinks that the Japanese boy is annoying her. Jong-il and the girl's reaction may seem to be extreme. However, it reflects the reality in which female Korean school students wearing Korean costume as school uniforms have often been a target of curious gazes, ill-will and harassment as a result of Japanese prejudice. The original novel contains a passage, 'she in Chima-chogori (Korean costume) is burdened on her thin shoulders with the North Korea's terrorist acts, kidnapping issues, suspicion over the nuclear development'.[7] Every time some conflict occurs between Japan and North Korea, the hostility towards North Korea has commonly been directed towards Korean schoolgirls, who are visibly (North) Korean by virtue of their Korean-style school uniform. The possibility of another cross-cultural romance leads to tragedy, as the boy happens to kill Jong-il after tussling. Thus, Jong-il's dream of becoming a Korean-school teacher does not materialize. This, in turn, implies that the possibility of positive multiple identifications or cultural syncretism is also crushed. In doing so, the film may

7 Kazuki Kaneshiro, *Go!* (Tokyo, 2000), p. 147.

also be taken to imply that there is no place for the hybrid culture and identity embodied by Jong-il in Japanese (including zainichi) society.

It must be noted here that the film criticizes the Korean (more appropriately North Korean) ethno-national essentialism embodied by Sugihara's and Jong-il's teacher known as 'Satan Kim' at the North Korean ethnic school. Satan Kim is an extreme North Korean ethno-nationalist and sadist whose hobby is punishing students who use Japanese at the school. In one scene, Sugihara's classmate Wonsu is tipped off by another student about using Japanese, and is hit by Satan Kim. As I mentioned earlier, he is also furious at Sugihara's decision to transfer to Japanese high school. These scenes may reveal and criticize the authoritarian and essentialist nature of the system of North Korean education. However, their function as self-reflexive criticisms of zainichi society more generally is rather ambiguous, since such criticism is targeted exclusively at this figure of North Korean authority. Similarly, Sugihara's father's excessive violence is simply reduced to paternal love rather than as a means of criticizing the Confucian-based male (that is, father)-dominated patriarchal family system.

The scenes in which Wonsu is scolded by Satan Kim and another teacher for using Japanese may be funny yet, at the same time, they invite us to consider the relationship or friction between zainichi and their mother language. The conversation between Satan Kim and Wonsu during the class (called a 'self-criticism class' as students are required to criticise their use of Japanese language) is as follows. (Words in italics are spoken in Japanese and the rest is in Korean.)

Satan Kim: What did you say?
Wonsu: *'Really wanna take a shit'.* I felt, *'I really wanna take a shit'.*
            As *'I really wanna take shit'*, I said, *'I really wanna take a shit'.*
            What's wrong with saying *'I really wanna take shit'.*
            ... Well, how should I say when *'I really wanna take shit'.*
Satan Kim: I want to defecate.
Wonsu: That does not sound what I felt. So I used *'I really wanna take shit'* in Japanese.

In another self-criticism class, Wonsu is again caught by another teacher.

Wonsu: Then, how should I say, *'Get me a porn mag'*?
Teacher: Would you please buy me an adult magazine?
Wonsu: It does not sound what I want, so I said, *'Get me a porn mag'.*

What these conversations indicate is the distance between zainichi and their so-called 'mother tongue'. While for many zainichi without ethnic education, Korean is no more than an 'imagined' mother language, those who go/went to ethnic school possess considerable fluency in Korean. Yet, as Wonsu's remarks suggest, even zainichi with fluent Korean, face the gap between their

Korean language and their trivial daily experiences and feelings. This is partly because the Korean spoken and taught at Korean ethnic schools is old-fashioned and solemn and, therefore, unsuitable for young people's resort to slang. However, more importantly, what these scenes comically demonstrate is that it is an undeniable fact that it is Japanese not Korean that govern the deeper parts of zainichi daily lives. To govern zainichi life does not simply mean that zainichi are more exposed to Japanese language in the external environment. Japanese as a governing language is internalized deeply into the body, or as Wonsu's example suggests, it may be closely bound up with experiences and feelings related to basic instincts such as excretion and sex.

The director, Yukisada Isao has commented in an interview that one of the main reasons for filming *Go!* was to make the Japanese aware of the discrimination against zainichi.[8] Although it is true that *Go!* deals with discrimination against zainichi, it is treated in a superficial and excessive manner that fails to examine covert prejudice and racism. For the majority of viewers, the discrimination presented in *Go!* will be seen to be confined to a small number of extreme racists, not a prevailing social problem that requires self-examination. In other words, the viewers do not have to identify themselves with racists. It does not mean, however, that they then identify themselves with Sugihara, as the cool but poor victim. For Sugihara remains as the object to be seen by the sympathetic, yet responsibility-free, gaze of the viewers.

Sugihara's position as an object is confirmed by the fact that Sugihara is often deprived of point-of-view shots. This leads us to question Sugihara's position as the speaking subject. For instance, in one scene, one of Sugihara's few Japanese friends, Kato, suggests that he come to his birthday party. Kato is standing close behind Sugihara and two girls are playing with a video camcorder behind them. As Kato says 'there will be lots of cuties', he turns Sugihara round so he can see the girls. However, rather than taking Sugihara's (and Kato's) point of view and showing the girls from the front, the next shot captures the two girls' lower halves from behind. The foreground of the screen is therefore dominated by the girl's legs and their knickers seen under their skirts while Kato and Sugihara are seen in the background. The girls' legs and knickers are not what Sugihara is seeing while, at the same time, it is not a shot intended to highlight his presence. Rather, it seems to be more like a self-display or playful intervention on the part of the director.

In the sequence near the end of the film discussed earlier, Sugihara gives a passionate speech about his identity and his anger towards Japanese (including Sakurai's) racism. Here, despite his monologue, his position as a speaking 'subject' is rather ambiguous. Although there are several reverse shots of Sakurai looking at Sugihara, the camera keeps capturing Sugihara. This seems to encourage viewers to identify themselves with Sakurai while Sugihara

8 Cited in White, 'Zainichi Korean identity'.

becomes a speaking object to be seen. Moreover, rather than being scared by Sugihara's anger, Sakurai calmly looks at his eyes. We see here Sugihara's fierce glare in close-up. Sakurai then says that she loved these (that is, angry) eyes and it was when Sugihara was kicking his team-mates at the basketball court that she saw this angry look and was impressed by it. For Sakurai, how he looks seems to be more important than what he says. Here, Sugihara is presented as a speaking and angry, yet, cool object, rather than as a speaking subject who criticizes and challenges the racism with which he is confronted.

Henry Louis Gates, Jr, one of the leading cultural critics on multicultural and African-American issues, has observed, 'Once scorned, now exalted ... It takes all the fun out of being oppositional when someone hands you a script and says, "Be oppositional, please – you look so cute when you're angry"'.⁹ Gates' comment seems to be useful in understanding how Sugihara or, more pertinently, the zainichi issues are treated in the film. It also helps to raise the question of the extent to which the director Yukisada is, in fact, attempting to make a film, as he said, which makes the Japanese aware of racism.

As I have already discussed, the discrimination of zainichi is treated in a very superficial way and Sugihara's position as speaking subject is unstable and ambiguous, with the camera repeatedly capturing him as an object. Moreover, throughout the film, the flashy and stylish cinematic style often overwhelms the zainichi theme or turns it into a fashionable 'spectacle'. In this respect, it can be argued that, rather than engaging with the zainichi issue, Yukisada seems to use the 'zainichi issue' as raw material with which he indulges his artistic and creative narcissism. To use Gates' commentary as a metaphor, Yukisada may be an artist who gives a script to the actor who has recently become a trendy object and asks him/her to adopt an oppositional pose for him. However, what he is interested in may be neither the actor, nor his social stance, but the manifestation of his own creative talents or skills.

Here the word narcissism is being used in a popular sense as a self-love or self-indulgence and, in this respect, the film's main character Sugihara also displays some narcissistic aspects. Sugihara's Korean identity alternates between self-loathing and self-love. He is apparently uncomfortable with and angry about being labelled as zainichi but, at the same time, he seems to be intoxicated by his oppositional tragic hero status. It is a form of self-love in the sense that it glorifies his self-image as a poor young man who alone fights against prejudice and discrimination. To refer to Gates Jr again, Sugihara is a rebel being asked to assume an oppositional pose. However, rather than rejecting the script and the patronizing remark saying 'you look cute when you are angry', he is intoxicated with his scripted oppositional role and the flattery and falls into his own narcissism. What is important here is that the two narcissisms of the director and character seem to complement and serve each other.

9 Henry Louis Gates, Jr, *Loose canons* (New York, 1992), p. 185.

The character Sugihara is not a creation of the director Yukisada, alone. As I mentioned earlier, *Go!* is based on an autobiographical novel of a young zainichi writer, Kaneshiro. In this respect, it is safe to say that Sugihara's narcissism is the reflection of that of Kaneshiro. Or, more appropriately, Kaneshiro's narcissism creates Sugihara, a cool rebellious hero in his self-image. Moreover, Kaneshiro's narcissism may reflect, to some extent, the narcissism shared by many (especially male) zainichi population who tend to indulge themselves in a victim status *vis-à-vis* Japanese society, but who are often blind to the problems within zainichi society, such as the patriarchal family system. Although Sugihara's father may represent, to some extent, a violent father (one of the most often cited problems within the zainichi family system), his paternal love is emphasized much more. Similarly, although *Go!* (both the film and novel) contains strong criticism of the authoritarian North Korean ethnic education, its capacity to generate self-reflexive criticism of the zainichi community is ambivalent, given that it may be seen simply as a criticism of North Korea, long considered the biggest enemy of, and threat to, Japan.

As such the film *Go!* is a text containing at least three narrational voices: that of the main character, Sugihara, the film's director, Yukisada, and the author of the original novel, Kaneshiro. However, rather than critically engaging with the issue of zainichi, all of them fall into their own narcissism and their narcissisms intersect and reinforce each other. In this respect, *Go!* provides a good example of contemporary Japanese 'cosmetic multiculturalism'. 'Cosmetic multiculturalism' is a term proposed by Tessa Morris-Suzuki. Although there has been a trend in recent Japan to praise cultural diversity under the banner of multiculturalism, as the word 'cosmetic' suggests Morris-Suzuki considers Japanese multiculturalism to be superficial and often no more than a disguised form of nationalism. While cultural diversity is praised and 'other' cultures become the object of economic consumption, this only serves to exemplify Japan's generosity towards, and capacity to accommodate, 'other' cultures.[10] In *Go!*, the zainichi 'other' embodied in the character Sugihara remains a trendy object of spectacle and the director Yukisada seem to uses the theme of zainichi as a device for materializing the director's narcissistic use of cinematic form. Although it is not uncommon and certainly not wrong that some filmmakers are concerned more with formal issues than narrative substance (whether or not this involves socio-political issues), like cosmetic multiculturalism, what the director celebrates is himself rather than 'other' cultures. Moreover, it is also a good example of how minority groups often unwittingly take part in the cosmetic operation of Japanese multiculturalism by playing a 'scripted' role and falling into their own form of essentialism.

---

10 Tessa Morris-Suzuki, '*"Posutokoroniarizmu" no imi wo megutte*' ('Discussion over the meanings of "post-colonialism"'), *Gendai Shiso*, 29:9 (2001), p. 185.

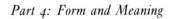

Part 4: Form and Meaning

The films of Andrei Tarkovsky: between the spiritual and the ecological

JOHN DARA WALDRON

In *The films of Krzysztof Kieslowski: the liminal image*, Joseph G. Kickasola anecdotally reflects on the nature of 'style' in the films of Andrei Tarkovsky:

> While discussing Tarkovsky at the Society of Cinema Studies Conference in 2002, a colleague confessed that he was never able to teach Tarkovsky's 'style' in a truly productive way. For instance, if there was a sumptuous visual of a tree-lined hill in a Tarkovsky film, he never felt able to articulate the full effect of the image.[1]

Kickasola situates this anecdote within a discussion of the spiritual in film. The anecdote underlines a difficulty in assessing technique, style or an aesthetic. Considering the style of filmmakers such as Robert Bresson and Kryzysztof Kieslowski, Kickasola argues that Tarkovsky's deployment of the spiritual is equally complex. The aim of this chapter is to explore the nature of this complexity by addressing the dialectical relation between the spiritual and the ecological in Tarkovsky's films. The first section of this chapter will address the spiritual impulse, examining the recurring motif of levitation in Tarkovsky's films. The second section will address the role of the ecological in Tarkovsky's films, while the last section will seek to delineate a space between these categories in response to the initial inquiry into Tarkovsky's style.

THE SPIRITUAL

The climax in three of Tarkovsky's films consists of a levitation – either a couple levitating or a partner gazing upon the other in levitation. To levitate means to float momentarily above the earth, unbound by gravity. As a climax, it evokes a spiritual impulse – in Christian theology the capacity to dissociate the self from the material (or for St Augustine, the capacity to withdraw from the world of action) – as it reaches a transcendent moment. When discussing

1 Joseph G. Kickasola, *The films of Kryzysztof Kieslowski: the liminal image* (New York, 2004), p. xiv.

the notion of transcendence, Paul Schrader has argued that the 'transcendental style is simply this: a representative filmic form which expresses the
Transcendent',[2] but Schrader's emphasis on 'transcendental' and 'style' is contradictory: style is a temporal constraint, at the mercy of fashion, the transcendental is permanent. Susan Sontag is the inspiration for Schrader's analysis of style, and it is not surprising that Sontag addresses style in her essay
entitled 'Spiritual style in the films of Robert Bresson'[3] using terms such as
'style' and 'spirit' in a similar fashion. Her analysis, drawing from traditional
theological sources, defines the spiritual moment *as* grace:

> Consciousness of self is the 'gravity' that burdens the spirit: the sur-
> passing of the consciousness of self is 'grace', or spiritual lightness.[4]

Grace is the lightness of spirit penetrating the body, an example of which is the
levitation scene in *Solaris* (1972). The scene occurs after the deceased Hari
(Nathalya Bondorchuk) reappears on the planet Solaris, offering Kris (Donatis
Banionis) the possibility of redemption. In the levitation scene Kris overcomes
'the gravity that burdens the spirit'. Having relived his earlier mistakes, he
accepts 'grace' and levitates. *Mirror* (1975), Tarkovsky's next film, reveals a
similar impulse. In the earring scene, the Narrator's mother Marousia
(Margarita Terekhova) visits a neighbour to trade her earrings for food to feed
her children. Just as the colour imagery of the scene changes to black and
white, Marousia's husband, who had been fighting in World War II, returns
home. As he gazes upon his wife, the father switches his gaze towards the
camera as it tracks towards him. Tarkovsky then cuts to the mother levitating above the bed, her bodily weight reduced to zero (a metaphor for the lightness of spirit experienced in the spiritual moment) – with the levitation, as
white doves fly about the room, signifying a fulfilment of the spiritual impulse.

   Tarkovsky's next two films, *Stalker* (1979) and *Nostalgia* (1983), fail to
utilize this now recurring motif. The motif is used again in Tarkovsky's last
film *The Sacrifice* (1986). *The Sacrifice* is the most traditionally Christian of
Tarkovsky's films, although the levitation scene is set against an array of pagan
motifs: fire, water, the sky, the trembling earth. In mature Tarkovskian style,
the film opens with a nine-a-half-minute take of a green pasture overlooking
the sea. Alexander (Erland Johansson), the protagonist, is planting a Japanese
tree while discussing issues of a metaphysical nature with the local postman,
Otto (Allan Edwall) (a retired teacher who has mystic tendencies). Tarkovsky's
use of the long take enables symbolic associations to develop between knowledge and the earth (the tree is a recurring motif in Tarkovsky's films suggesting natural wisdom) and paganism and ritual. In a later scene Alexander

2 Paul Schrader, *The transcendental style in Ozu, Bresson, Dreyer* (New York, 1972), pp 8–9.   3
Susan Sontag, *Against interpretation* (New York, 1996), pp 178–95.   4 Ibid., p. 193.

will have a premonition of nuclear war and will make a pact with God in order to save his son 'Little Man' (Tommy Kjellqvist). He also turns to Otto for advice. Alexander is advised by Otto to visit a Witch, Maria, whom he is told will offer him spiritual sustenance. After having spent an evening with Maria (Gudrun Gisladottir), and bearing his soul, the levitation scene occurs. Heavy green filters are used by the cinematographer Sven Nykvist to dramatise the moment in which Maria (the Witch) and Alexander levitate above the bed in sexual union – the lightness of the experience, the couple transcending the earthly pull of gravity, suggesting the fulfilment of a spiritual impulse.

Susan Sontag argues that Bresson's austere spiritual style is a reflection of the 'consciousness of self' in his films – a movement towards the relief of 'interior drama'.[5] The relief as dénouement occurs in an aesthetic in which the expressive features superfluous to the action are rejected. Grace occurs when everything *but* the spirit is excluded. Sontag develops her argument by suggesting Bresson's form offers a rejection of the psychological *tout court*. If psychology prevails, as in psychological realism, then characters dominate the art form. When domination such as this occurs the spectator will most possibly identify with 'characters' at the expense of 'form':

> The emotional distance typical of Bresson's films seems to exist for a different reason altogether: because all identification with characters, deeply conceived, is an impertinence – an affront to the mystery that is human actions and the human heart.[6]

Bresson seeks to prevent this over-identification with characters through a style devoid of fantasy and psychology. Thus, while a lack of psychological motivation in Bresson's characters may result in uncertainty, it is precisely this uncertainty, Sontag tells us, that is the intention of Bresson's aesthetic:

> The 'interior drama' which Bresson seeks to depict does not mean psychology. In realistic terms the motives of Bresson's characters are hidden, sometimes downright incredible.[7]

Grace, in this respect, consists of an 'incredible' alleviation from the gravity of life and for Bresson the brevity of grace occurs through a process of elimination that develops into a 'spiritual style'. By eliminating the decorative and inessential, the moment of grace is suggested, evoked, rarely forced. In Tarkovsky, the moment of grace has a literal purpose: the moment of transcendence is directly felt in levitation. Tarkovsky's aesthetic impulse, however, is towards the decorative, psychological, fantastical event. It is defined, fur-

5 Sontag, *Interpretation*, p. 193. 6 Ibid., p. 181. 7 Ibid., p. 188.

thermore, by features which emerge as a 'dynamic' attempt to differentiate 'art' from the real:

> In reality the concept of things that 'have to be' is incompatible with art. A work of art, of whatever art form, is constructed only according to its own principles, and is based on its own inner, dynamic stereoscope.[8]

Tarkovsky's scepticism with what 'has to be' suggests fantasy is central to his films. The novel *Solaris* on which the film is based concerns a human inability to conceive of alien spirit, but in the film Tarkovsky explores the spiritual impulse at the heart of human consciousness. In contrast to the spirit evoked in an alien context in Lem's novel, spirit is presented as a fantastical event in Tarkovksy's film version of *Solaris*. The spiritual, suggested, hinted at in Bresson's films, is expressed in an abundant and literal way in the film. The levitation is abundant in the sense that special effects and camera tricks are used by Tarkovsky to 'decorate' the spiritual moment; it is also literal insofar as the 'moment' itself is interpreted 'directly' without metaphor and metonymy.

Within the terms of this debate, Bresson's 'spiritual style' emanates from 'form that perfectly expresses and accompanies what he wants to say'.[9] Bresson's films *Pickpocket* (1959), *Mouchette* (1967) and *Au Hasard Balthazar* (1966) are examples of this 'form' in its most unexpressive, austere realization. In contrast, Tarkovsky's aesthetic oscillates between grace expressed in the form of levitation in *Solaris*, *Mirror* and *The Sacrifice* and the earthly, ecological 'form' of *The Sacrifice* and *Stalker*. In Christian doctrine, 'grace' is seen – in metaphorical terms – to involve floating above the earth, shedding bodily and material weight. However, because Tarkovsky expresses this experience literally in certain films the spiritual experience occurs as a fantasy – whereby the subject shown actually transcending the 'earth' – while in others the earth must have an empowering effect on the subject, quelling the fantastical impulse. *Solaris* is the first Tarkovsky film to deploy this spiritual impulse. The levitation presents Kris and Hari rising above the earth: with the facial image of Kris's mother interchanging with Hari's. The audience is liable to feel Kris is fantasizing about his mother (unconsciously), as a response to the guilt he feels towards Hari. However the resentment felt towards Hari for generating guilt (compounded by her suicide) may also be felt. As the characters levitate, the moment is fantastical with the separate images of mother and lover merging as one. The spiritual moment consists of Kris 'traversing the fantasy'.

An equally complex use of fantasy to suggest the spiritual occurs following what has become known as 'the earring scene' in *Mirror*. *Mirror* makes use of newsreels and documentary footage and Graham Petrie and Vida T. Johnson

---

8 Andrey Tarkovsky, *Time within time: the diaries, 1970–1986* (London, 1994), p. 369.   9 Ibid., p. 180.

suggest that the historical, the hardship of the Russian experience during World War Two, constitutes the central issue in the scene.[10] However, the return of the father at the end of the scene, when the mother levitates above the bed, introduces a fantastical event, which acts as a supplement to the flash-back memories contained in the film.[11] The change from colour to the black-and-white levitation suggests this is also a spiritual moment. Two points support this view. First of all, it is unlikely the father returned from the War at any time (as is noted in the interviews with Tarkovsky's family recorded by Petrie and Johnson), suggesting that the levitation is a fantasy (without any basis in the real). This leads on to the question of who then is fantasizing? The likelihood, as Petrie and Johnson suggest, is that the Narrator is fantasizing about being the father (creating and adding this scene as a fictional ploy), offering spiritual grace to his mother in the form of levitation.[12] If this is the case, the scene assumes a retroactive quality, imposing fiction on a real-life event. The mother receives 'grace' but the reception of grace is a fictional rendition of the spiritual impulse, an impulse, within Lacanian terms, to 'traverse the fantasy'. In psychoanalysis, Jacques Lacan sees this hallucinatory impulse as the mainstay of desire:

> The function of desire is a last residuum of the effect of the signifier in the subject. *Desidero* is the Freudian *cogito*. It is necessarily there that the essential of the primary process is established. Note well what Freud says of the field, in which the impulse is satisfied essentially by hallucination.[13]

From this exposition of desire, one can take the hallucinatory impulse as a reason why the Tarkovskian Narrator experiences the spiritual as 'the essential of the primary process'. In *The Sacrifice* the divide between 'fantasy' (as hallucinatory) and the real reaches an almost impenetrable level, leading Petrie and Johnson to argue:

> It is difficult – even impossible – to interpret many of the characters of the film in purely, or primarily, naturalistic terms, this is even more true of the film's 'action', especially its 'central events': the nuclear catastrophe and Alexander's sacrifice(s). Here Tarkovsky blurs even further than in previous films the distinction between dream and reality, actuality and hallucination, and the visual and aural coding that had earlier provided some clues for separating these out now becomes thoroughly ambiguous.[14]

10 Graham Petrie and Vida T. Johnson, *The films of Andrei Tarkovsky: a visual fugue* (Bloomington, 1994), pp 128–9. 11 Ibid. 12 Ibid. 13 Jacques Lacan, *The four fundamental concepts of psychoanalysis* (London, 1994), p. 154. 14 Petrie and Johnson, *The films of Andrei Tarkovsky*, p. 174.

Petrie and Johnson make the further point that the dichotomy is blurred even
more when the encounter with the Witch (a sign of pagan ritual and materi-
alism as much as Christianity in the film) is considered – an encounter in
which the relationship between impulses is even further complicated. The
pagan symbolism of the Witch (confounding critics of the film since its release)
conflicts with the spiritual symbolism of the levitation, forming a dual impulse.
The pagan symbolism of the 'earth' can now be associated with the 'modern'
ecological theme of 'saving the earth'.

THE ECOLOGICAL

Between the spiritual – the release of the self from the burden of earthly material life in fantasy – and the ecological – the deep-felt sense of earthly bond-
ing – there is, in *The Sacrifice* and *Stalker*, a conflict weighted towards the
ecological. The ecological impulse can be defined as an anti-religious movement bent on 'saving the earth' but, even with this definition intact, Slavoj
Žižek argues that an accompanying, emergent sense of spirituality can be identified in certain scenes in these films.[15] Žižek addresses Tarkovskian spirituality in the following analysis:

> The inert insistence of time as Real, rendered paradigmatically in
> Tarkovsky's famous slow five-minute tracking or crane shots, is what
> makes Tarkovsky so interesting for a materialist reading: without this
> inert texture he would just be another Russian religious obscurantist.
> That is to say, in our standard ideological tradition, the approach to
> spirit is perceived as elevation, as getting rid of the burden of weight,
> of the gravitational pull which binds us to the earth, of cutting links
> with material inertia and starting to 'float freely'; in contrast to this
> in Tarkovsky's universe one attains spirituality only via intense direct
> physical contact with the earth (or stagnant water).[16]

Zizek draws on the swamp scene in *Stalker* as the template for his analysis
but he argues that in *Stalker* the 'spiritual' is transfigured by a spirituality
attained 'via direct physical contact with the earth'.[17] While the spiritual is
most likely a fantastical moment in *Solaris* and *Mirror*, Žižek sees spirituality
attained in the universe of *Stalker*, as he puts it, via the opposite. The plot of
Stalker concerns a group of travellers navigating through a Zone to find a
Room which offers to grant an 'innermost wish' (the 'wish' a metaphor for
permanent spiritual well-being). When the group reach the Room they decide

15 Slavoj Žižek, *The fright of real tears: Krzysztop Kieslowski between theory and post-theory*
(London, 2001), p. 102.   16 Ibid.   17 Ibid.

not to enter. Prior to this decision – in what has become known as the swamp scene – the Stalker narrates a story from the Gospels. The intersection of narrative and image highlights the relationship between the ecological and spiritual themes. The Stalker tells of the apostles meeting Jesus after the resurrection and of how they fail to recognize their saviour. During this narration the camera tracks, in close-up, the Writer's body. In the story the apostles' failure to recognize Christ suggests a failure to believe, to see. At this point in the story the Writer abruptly opens his eyes, suggesting he now has the capacity to see. The scene draws on images and signs David Gillespie suggests are typical of the mature Soviet cinema:[18] the landscape of the Zone is an industrial wasteland overwrought with natural growth, the decaying icon of the Madonna beside the decadent symbol of the needle, and the Stalker's meditation on the Utopian potential of music. Aside from these images and signs suggesting the failed Utopian potential of 1920s revolutionary Russia is the space of the Zone, used by Tarkovsky as a metaphor for the earth. This space evokes the nineteenth-century Romantic Movement's emphasis on nature and, when coupled with a story from the gospels, is used to emphasize the spiritual sustenance needed for a return to the earth. The ecological moment, occurring when the Writer awakens from the swamp, is a moment in which a rejection of the impulse to fantasize, the spiritual, derives from the spirituality of the earth.

By the end, the 'innermost wish' of each traveller is unfulfilled but the group have confronted the natural landscape of the earth, transforming their individual private fantasies into a public project, attaining, as Žižek argues, lasting spirituality. The spiritual is a fantastical event in *Solaris* and *Mirror*, but countering this is a 'spirituality' which derives from the 'inert texture' of the earth. The group's encounter with this 'texture' can be read, in Lacanian terms, as an encounter with the Real:

> The real has to be sought beyond the dream – in what the dream has enveloped, hidden from us, behind the lack of representation of which there is only one representative. This is the real that governs our activities more than any other and it is psychoanalysis which designates it for us.[19]

That which has only one representative for Lacan, the Real, is presented by another in Tarkovsky: the earth. The dialectic of dream and real is dominated by one or the other in his first six films but in Tarkovsky's last film, *The Sacrifice*, the two are equally present. The plot is based on Alexander attempting to 'save the earth'. At the beginning of the film Alexander fantasizes about dispensing with language and communicating directly with God. On the one

18 David Gillespie, *Russian cinema* (London, 2003), p. 5.   19 Lacan, *Concepts*, p. 60.

hand, this is a plea to God to save him in a time of need, by allowing him to dispense with the symbolic. On the other, it is an attempt to resuscitate the symbolic. This duality generates a question as to whether Alexander in the film is fantasizing about the spiritual or encountering the Real: the latter as the earthly experience which transforms the Word. To connect directly with the 'earth', to go beyond the dream, Alexander must experience the earth directly which is paralleled by Tarkovsky's attempt formally to unify fantasy and the Real. The problem for the viewer is that this unity is related to Maria, who is also a Witch in the film.

Maria, the Witch, is a character who has links with the pagan 'earth' yet her home is decorated with Christian 'spiritual' symbols in the film. When Alexander visits Maria, the 'spiritual' moment for which Tarkovskian heroes strive occurs in what is usually a fantasy scene: the levitation. Alexander's engagement with the 'earth' is felt in the scenes prior to his visit when the shading and colour of the landscape externalize the hero's 'interior drama'. The difficulty now is maintaining equilibrium between the spiritual and the ecological, particularly as the levitation is experienced *with* the Witch. It is hard to approach this point in *The Sacrifice* without the character of Maria, the Witch, causing confusion. Petrie and Johnson draw attention to the pagan significance of a 'Witch' in Western mythology but also, inform us of how 'in the Russian sense of the word' a 'Witch' is someone who knows.[20] The ambiguous Witch reflects the ambiguity of spiritual and ecological dimensions in the film. The Witch is close to the earth (in a pagan context), but also spiritually aware, a 'holy fool'. At the end of *The Sacrifice* an ambulance takes Alexander away and 'Little Man' is heard saying 'in the beginning there was the Word, why is that Papa?' The statement, and accompanying question to the father, suggests Alexander's encounter with the Witch and resuscitates he and his son's relationship to the Word. Alexander's actions are therefore spiritually related to the Word. Thus the Witch must have spiritual powers. This ambiguity is confusing but the film can be viewed through a Žižekian lens as an attempt to associate spirituality with the earth. This then is an attempt to consolidate a position developed in previous films. When Alexander sets fire to his family home, the Japanese kimono that he wears suggests two points which might clarify the ending of the film. First of all the symbols of ying and yang reflect Tarkovsky's attempt to unify spiritual and ecological impulses (ying being the spiritual in the film, yang the ecological). Secondly, this unity suggests the encounter with the Witch is positive. This is evident in the 'form' of the film: the shading that dominates Alexander's plight as it becomes apparent returns to 'full' colour at the end. This change suggests the 'act' has generated an enlightened moment. 'Little Man' is offered the symbolic, the spiritual Word.

20 Petrie and Johnson, *The films of Andrei Tarkovsky*, p. 175.

BETWEEN THE SPIRITUAL AND THE ECOLOGICAL

Tarkovsky gave a number of hints concerning the meaning of Alexander's sacrifice in his writings, and considerable debate has arisen concerning the meaning of sacrifice in Tarkovsky's films. Žižek addresses the sacrifice, not just in
The Sacrifice but in Tarkovsky's films as a whole, as an event which can, and
perhaps should be, considered intentionally meaningless:

> What happens if we read the Tarkovskian sacrificial gesture in the
> opposite way: what if we interpret the Tarkovskian sacrificial gesture
> as a very elementary ideological operation, as a desperate strategy of
> beating the meaninglessness of existence by its own means i.e. of
> engendering meaning – of overcoming the unbearable Otherness of
> meaningless cosmic contingency – through a gesture that is itself
> meaningless?[21]

The sacrificial event has an ambiguous meaning in *The Sacrifice* which Zizek
believes is intentionally meaningless.[22] However, because of the difficulty in
finding a definite meaning for the event, the film is considered the most flawed
– in terms of 'plot' – of Tarkovsky's films. The general thrust, both in the
content and form of *The Sacrifice*, may be read as an attempt on Tarkovsky's
part to unify dialectically the spiritual and ecological themes which dominate
the other films. The levitation scene, an example of this, is suggestive of spiritual grace, but is set against pagan images (the egg as a symbol of wholeness,
the affirmative body, the landscape) to emphasize the positioning of the earth,
the ecological, in Tarkovsky's films. In this way, the film may be seen to designate a filmic space where fantasy and the real, the spiritual and ecological,
merge. *The Sacrifice* draws together the images which dominate the other films:
the levitation, the looming landscapes (typical of the Russian cinema), the
colour shading (altering the dominant signs of cinema), and the earth, the pivotal object from which man is borne and will return. Accordingly, the film
represents an attempt to bring together impulses, spiritual and ecological, characteristic of the previous films.

In the conclusion to his book of essays about his films, *Sculpting in Time*,
Tarkovsky argues that the nineteenth-century Romantic aesthetic concerned
art that embodied:

> An ideal: it was an example of the perfect balance between the moral
> and material principles, a demonstration of the fact that such a bal-
> ance is not a myth existing only in the realm of ideology.[23]

21 Žižek, *Tears*, p. 106. 22 Ibid. 23 Andrei Tarkovsky, *Sculpting in time*, trans. Kitty Hunter-
Blair (Austin, TX, 1987), p. 238.

The ying and yang symbols on Alexander's kimono in *The Sacrifice* are a reminder to the spectator of the moral and the material, defined in this essay as the spiritual and ecological, which the films as a whole attempt to balance even if this proves unachievable (as an absolute). For, as Tarkovsky tells us, his 'aesthetic' is based not on what 'has to be' but on an 'inner, dynamic stereoscope'.[24]

24 Tarkovsky, *Time within time*, p. 369.

Music, modernism, and modernization in Djibril Diop Mambety's *Touki Bouki*

ALEXANDER FISHER

From the mid-1980s onwards there has been a steady increase of scholastic interest in film music, motivated in part by the predominant visual bias of film studies practice. Such scholarship has tended to concentrate on Hollywood cinema, its theoretical locus being the 'unheard melody', an idea developed in the 1980s by Claudia Gorbman in which the classical Hollywood score functions as an invisible cueing device with which audiences engage at an unconscious level and which bonds the viewer to texts by assisting his/her identification with the characters and events on screen.[1] However, the attention given to the film score has only just begun to extend beyond the boundaries of Hollywood and European cinemas, and film studies lacks an understanding of the relationships between music and image in what might be called non-Western cinemas. In the following paper I would like to consider the use of music in Djibril Diop Mambety's landmark feature *Touki Bouki/ The Hyena's Journey* (Senegal, 1973), which has been characterized as a modernist text and which almost always attracts a passing mention for its use of Josephine Baker's voice. However, previous discussions have barely extended beyond talking about the music's lyrics and Mambety's intrusive editing of the soundtrack. Consequently the structural complexities of the music's use, as well as the connotations of its musical idiom, created by the organization of its vocal and instrumental as well as rhythmic and melodic elements, have been overlooked. This has lead critics simply to pigeon-hole the film's use of music within a notion of 'modernism', whereby the oppositional aspects of its abrupt editing are accorded greater significance than the specificities of its organization.

Furthermore, the 'modernism' label as applied by critics has tended simply to mean 'departures from the classical Hollywood mode', which overlooks the specificities of the modernity from which particular 'modernisms' might emerge. Other readings of the film have attempted an Africanist interpretation of its narrative, sidestepping the question of modernism altogether. I suspect, however, that the tendency to read the film either within purely Africanist terms or against the classical Hollywood paradigm derives from the prevalence of the opposition between tradition and modernity in literary and

---

1 Claudia Gorbman, *Unheard melodies: narrative film music* (London, 1987).

film studies. However, insofar as the notion of 'tradition' is itself a child of 'modernity', against which 'modernity' defines itself, the interdependency of the two concepts suggests that this is an opposition that is inherently flawed. I will argue therefore that an understanding of the music in *Touki Bouki* exposes this flaw, demonstrating how a close analysis of the film's musical components not only enhances our understanding of the film's location within Senegal's encounter with modernization (as opposed to modern*ism*), but furthermore reveals a thematic engagement with the ways in which these encounters are structured. In this respect, film studies' failure to scrutinize music may be linked to the tendency to overlook a level of complexity in the text's negotiations with – and location within – modernization that is played out via a contrapuntal play of music and image.

The two potential interpretive approaches for the film described above have been outlined by N. Frank Ukadike (although he uses the term *avant-garde* where another critic may well use the term 'modernist'). Ukadike suggests that both readings of the film are shaped by the film's breaks from narrative convention:

> [T]he unconventional manner in which time, space, and events are juxtaposed compels one to appreciate the film as a non-narrative whose collage of cultural, political, and sexual imagery offers a wide array of connotative assumptions. For example, while non-African critics have read the film as an avant-gardist manipulation of reality, an Africanist analysis would attempt a reconfigurative reading that synthesises the narrative components and reads the images as representing an indictment of contemporary African life-styles and socio-political situations in disarray.[2]

Ukadike precludes the possibility that there may be thematic aspects of the film that may be understood without recourse to issues of narrative convention. Likewise, Malkmus and Armes discuss how 'Diop Mambety has devised a structure that fills out the spaces through which the protagonists pass with secondary characters, perhaps because traditional African approaches demand a link between hero and community, or perhaps, on the contrary, out of a purely modernist impulse to allow the narrative to generate itself'.[3] Ukadike and Armes/Malkmus invoke an apparent fissure between Africanist and modernist readings of the film, although both of these simply constitute different interpretive frameworks. From a modernist perspective, the film is a *modernist* response to Africa's encounter with *modernity* via colonialism and the globalizing effects of capitalism. Patrick Williams has provided such a reading of

2 N. Frank Ukadike, *Black African cinema* (Berkeley, 1994), p. 173.   3 Linda Malkmus and Roy Armes, *Arab and African filmmaking* (London, 1991), p. 191.

both *Touki Bouki* and Mambety's 1992 feature, *Hyènes/Hyenas* (Senegal). Suggesting that 'the slightly slower emergence of black African cinema meant that for some – but by no means all – directors the anatomizing of domestic failures was already a less interesting question than engagement with the West, and above all with the West in the shape of modernity',⁴ Williams goes on to describe the film as 'Mambety's own fiercely modernist negotiations with modernity', having defined modernism as 'the cultural response to modernity'.⁵ While *Touki Bouki* clearly *does* engage with Africa's encounter with the West, and with the apparently *modernising* aspects of this encounter, to employ modernism as an *interpretive framework*, and effectively graft on an understanding of the film via what is a (relatively crude) means of understanding a particular trend in Western cultural production sidesteps the specificities of the structures embodied within, for one, Mambety's cutting of the musical track. As I have already suggested, moder*nism* in film (as distinct from its engagement with issues of *modernity* or its *engagement with* modernist forms) in fact tends to mean 'departures from dominant (Hollywood) film practice'; therefore it would clearly be pointless to attempt to find meaning in *Touki Bouki*'s various visual and aural signs and symbols since their significance would lie in their apparent random-ness, emerging from 'a purely modernist impulse to allow the narrative to generate itself'. Likewise, Ukadike's suggested Africanist analysis itself is dependent on a break from convention, and is thus ultimately defined by its opposition to dominant film practice (in this context more likely to be defined as Western, rather than Hollywood). While the following analysis of the film will be closer in methodology to the Africanist 'reconfigurative' reading rather than a modernist interpretation, its motivation is propelled by a suspicion of such restrictive interpretive regimes and their dependence on notions of oppositionality.

Touki Bouki is a film concerned with two courting youngsters' escape from the precarious modernity of post-colonial Dakar. Mory (the male protagonist) decides they will flee their poverty and settle in Paris, travelling to the coast on his motorbike and taking a boat to France. While Mory initially leads the way, his partner Anta, an intellectually empowered woman who dresses in men's clothes and plans to go to university, gradually evolves into a more independent individual who is able to board the boat to France, while Mory panics and is unable to leave Senegal. The uncompleted journey from the slums to Paris via the unstable modernity of Dakar's city centre represents, for many critics (such as Williams and Malkmus and Armes), a quest for a utopian notion of modernity that is epitomized by Paris but which probably does not exist. Mory's decisive break for Paris occurs during a pivotal sequence in which

---

4 Patrick Williams, '"Entering and leaving modernity" – utopia and dystopia in Mambety's *Touki Bouki* and *Hyènes*' in Wendy Everett (ed.), *The seeing century* (Amsterdam, 2000), p. 125. 5 Williams, '"Entering and leaving modernity"', p. 127.

he leads Anta away on a roaring motorbike. All diegetic sound is then removed and, in the first of five occurrences on the soundtrack, Josephine Baker is heard singing 'Paris, Paris'. This is a light-hearted cabaret song which comes to represent, via its mildly distorted, 'crackling' sound (denoting an earlier vinyl recording), its French lyrics and its particular musical idiom (connoting Paris's, probably imaginary, 'golden age'), the utopian city that Mory and Anta seek, and which Mory will ultimately fail, to reach.

The repetitive 'song' we hear in the movie and the original recording from which it is borrowed are very different entities. Mambety utilizes two short sections of the original recording; we hear first a male group singing the words 'Paris, Paris, Paris' in a four-five second sample that is then repeated. This is followed by Josephine Baker singing the first two lines of the original song's chorus ('Paris, Paris, Paris, it's a corner of paradise on earth'). These two samples represent the entire content of the music in the scene, and they are repeated in this order several times. Thus the male voices singing 'Paris, Paris, Paris' (which represent a very small portion of the original recording) come to dominate what might be called the song's *refrain*, serving a pivotal function for Josephine Baker's voice whose use in this context more closely resembles that of the *verse* of the song. Thus the song's two (new) sections are heard in the form of b,a,b,a,b,a. The effect is rather like that of a gramophone stylus trapped in the groove of a vinyl disc (perhaps the ultimate example of the failure of modernity – the scientific phenomenon of sound reproduction becomes, literally, 'stuck'). While there is little structural resemblance between the two recordings, the qualities of the vocalist and the instrumentation (light orchestra of strings, woodwind and piano), and thus their idiomatic origins, remain evident.

This disruptive musical presence occurs against a narrative which unfolds in a fairly linear mode. Moreover, Mory and Anta's ride by motorbike is depicted in a way that may be aligned with the conventions of Hollywood cinema, with a mixture of front and rear mid-shots depicting the characters as they ride the bike, the environment in which they are located ('anywhere in Africa') being clearly visible, and the causal relationship of the shots closely representing the temporal linearity of events. Similarly, the way in which the sequence functions within the overall narrative may be aligned with such a notion of temporal linearity, providing a bridge between the inaction and the action of the characters following Mory's decision to leave for Paris, and as such propels the narrative, transporting the characters towards their goal. This temporal linearity may also be broadly aligned with classical Hollywood conventions, and the film's engagement with and exploitation of these conventions refers to the formal realism that characterizes classical Hollywood.[6]

6 David Bordwell, Janet Staiger and Kristin Thompson identify a 'Classical Hollywood cinema' which may be identified through set of stylistic norms that characterize Hollywood studio

This is not to say, of course, that the film never breaks from these conventions on visual and narrative levels; in fact the film is characterized by its frequent narrative non-sequiturs, the most prominent example being the film's opening section, in which images of cattle being slaughtered are combined with shots of Mory and Anta riding the motorbike to no apparent narrative purpose (again, these have generally been read within the terms of modernism).[7] However, the majority of the film, at the visual level and at the level of diegetic sound, is concerned with the passage of the two characters towards Paris. In the 'Paris, Paris' sequence, it is the apparent disruption of the music's temporal flow against the realist visual depiction of the couple that dislocates the spectator's identification with the characters and their personal goals and, as such, adds a level of distanciation that may be seen as constituting an authorial intervention. Thus the film may be (and indeed has been) seen as actively exploiting dominant cinematic conventions through its regular (or perhaps, more aptly, irregular) disturbance of them.

However, while the sequence does indeed represent a conscious disruption of cinematic convention and viewer expectation, this disruption is not only a means to provoke the distanciation of the spectator. For the abrupt cutting and re-ordering of the audio track also allow the music to acquire a multi-layered significance. At a fundamental level, as almost all readings of the film suggest, these devices serve to represent the characters' notion of Paris as a modern utopia. However, the abrupt editing distances the viewer from his or her previously acquired identification with the characters in their quest to reach this utopia. In being denied the comfort of the music's resolution, the viewer is pointed to an implied author, whose intervention occurs via the apparent distortion and re-ordering of a song that promises to tell of a city that resembles 'a corner of Paradise' but which is never allowed to complete its narrative. As such the notion of modernity embodied in the song's lyrics and musical genre is exposed as a mini-grand narrative of Western superiority. Thus the music acts as a precursor to the film's ending, in which Mory is unable to board the boat to France, and thus never reaches Paris. While his partner Anta does board, the implication is that the modernity she seeks simply does not exist. This in turn gives way to a new layer of significance that lies in the use of Josephine Baker's voice, pointing to a notion of modernity played out via a post-colonial or, more specifically, post-slavery narrative. (The viewer familiar with Baker will in turn be alerted to Baker's film roles in which she is exoticized as a primitive spectacle.)[8] As a result, the utopian modernity that

productions in *The classical Hollywood cinema: film style and mode of production to 1960* (London, 1985).   7 Although careful analysis of these apparent narrative 'fragments' may be interpreted as representing the psychological interiority of the characters, and as such may 'make sense' when subjected to such an interpretive regime.   8 For instance, in *Princess Tam Tam* (France, 1935). See Kathryn Kalinak, *Settling the score: music and the classical Hollywood film* (Madison, 2000).

the couple crave is exposed as a Western grand-narrative of superiority based
on a defining opposition of 'the modern' against 'the primitive'. Thus the
modern utopia of Paris defines itself via its contrast to the apparently failed
modernity of the slums (which both stand in for the West and Africa respec-
tively), and as such can be traced back to a history of Western exploitation of
the Third World which is expressed through the post-slavery narrative embodied in the figure Baker.

Moreover, at a formal level, the presence of a male backing-group to the
female voice of Baker, emphasized by Mambety's editing, points to a specific
reversing of the traditional gender hierarchy, a reversal that can be found in
abundance in the musical and cabaret genres and which alerts us to its place
within these practices (one need only think of Marilyn Monroe or Marlene
Dietrich for examples). The privileging of the female vocalist acts as a gesture towards the role that Anta is more easily able to assume than Mory;
towards the end of the film, as the couple book their boat tickets to France,
she is seen leaving the travel agents glamorously dressed, having dispensed
with her men's clothes in favour of some more conventionally feminine attire,
and is heard speaking in French rather than Wolof. When the travel agent
asks, 'Haven't I seen you before somewhere?', she replies 'In New York,
surely'. This dimension becomes particularly significant when considered
against what may be regarded as the more traditional ('un-modernized') gender
hierarchy referred to by the earlier images of the couple riding the motorbike;
the man is seen driving the bike, while the woman rides behind, being led
away by the male driver. This is further accentuated by the fact that Mory
makes the decision to leave for France shortly after they have had sexual intercourse, and as such leads Anta towards her 'modernized' (or maybe simply
'Westernized') future as her lover. The role reversal central to the song evokes
the objectification of women represented by the female lead vocalist. In the
case of Josephine Baker, as I have already stated, this takes on a racial-cul-
tural resonance when one considers the ways in which she was often objectified and exoticized on screen. Thus the empowerment of women that appears
to be represented in the music contrasts with the colonial perception of African
woman as subservient (in cultures where polygamy is often seen as the norm).
Yet Anta appears no less empowered in her Senegalese life (in that she is not
objectified), than apparently she will be should her dream be fulfilled. Her
break away from Mory at the end of the film could suggest that she is being
lead towards a life in which she will not only continue to be exploited for her
sexuality but also for her race. Thus, for the film, Anta does not leave tradition (as represented by the exploitation of women) for an opposing modernity (represented by the liberation of women), but simply travels between two
different ways of structuring two similar social hierarchies; in other words,
two different ways of organizing modernity. This echoes the song's repetition
and the sense of stasis it creates; thus 'modernist' notions of progress from

tradition to modernity are undermined and replaced with the idea that modernization affects all cultural formations and is simply organized in a multitude of diverse ways.

In conclusion, it can be seen that a more considered analysis of *Touki Bouki* that avoids the restrictive framework enforced by modernist and Africanist interpretive strategies and considers the implications of the film's use of music reveals a complex engagement with issues of modernization that are articulated via the relationship between gender and social hierarchies. This functions as an analogy for the wider issues of modernization, undermining the dominant tradition versus modernity debate and demonstrating that modernization progresses in ways and at rates specific to particular cultures. Moreover, the tendency towards restrictive readings of the film is in part a result of the general reluctance within film studies to tread within the highly specialized field of musical analysis, and as such modernist and Africanist readings provide a resort for the scholar who is competent in the heterogeneous field of cultural studies, but less comfortable in more specialized disciplines. As this brief venture into film and musicological analysis has suggested, *Touki Bouki*'s use of music neither represents a modernist nor Africanist oppositional gesture that acquires its meaning through its departures from dominant cinematic conventions, but rather forms part of a complex web of references which are invoked through the transformation and mutation of a particular musical idiom.

Designing asynchronous sound for film

LIZ GREENE

The sound designer, Randy Thom, writes as follows about the film director's attitude towards sound:

> Feature Film directors tend to oscillate between two wildly different states of consciousness about sound in their movies. On the one hand, they tend to ignore any serious consideration of sound (including music) throughout the planning, shooting and early editing. Then they suddenly get a temporary dose of religion when they realize that there are holes in the story, weak scenes and bad edits to disguise. Now they develop enormous and short-lived faith in the power and value of sound to make their movie watchable. Unfortunately it's usually too late, and after some vain attempts to stop a haemorrhage with a band-aid, the director's head drops, and sound cynicism rules again.[1]

This, however, is hardly an argument that applies to the films of David Lynch. As a result of his collaborations with the sound designer Alan Splet, David Lynch is unusual in his understanding of the role that sound may play in the cinema. Lynch first worked with Splet on the short film *The Grandmother* in 1969 and they subsequently collaborated on *Eraserhead* (1976), *The Elephant Man* (1980), *Dune* (1984) and *Blue Velvet* (1986). Splet was responsible for both the individual sound effects and the overall sound design on Lynch's films. In their films together, the soundtrack involves the mixing of many layers of sound, combining what has been recorded on set with sounds created in post-production. One of the most distinctive aspects of their work was the use of asynchrony in the creation of the soundtrack, and it is the mix of synchronous and asynchronous sound in films such as *Blue Velvet* with which the following discussion will be mainly concerned.

The importance of asynchronous sound was a key element of Eisenstein, Pudovkin and Alexandrov's manifesto 'A Statement on Sound'. They contended that sound could play a positive and creative role in the cinema, if used as a separate montage element. Their manifesto stated:

---

1 Thom quoted in Gianluca Sergi, *The Dolby era: film sound in contemporary Hollywood* (Manchester, 2004), p. 74.

THE FIRST EXPERIMENTAL WORK WITH SOUND MUST BE DIRECT-
ED ALONG THE LINE OF ITS DISTINCT NONSYNCHRONIZATION
WITH THE VISUAL IMAGES. And only such an attack will give the
necessary palpability which will later lead to the creation of an
ORCHESTRAL COUNTERPOINT of visual and aural images.[2]

Béla Balázs was later to describe the benefits of asynchrony for filmmakers as
follows:

> Asynchronous sound (that is, when there is a discrepancy between the
> things heard and seen in the film) can acquire considerable impor-
> tance. If the sound or voice is not tied up with a picture of its source,
> it may grow beyond the dimensions of the latter. Then it is no longer
> the voice or sound of some chance thing, but appears as a pro-
> nouncement of universal validity ... The surest means by which a
> director can convey the pathos or symbolic significance of sound or
> voice is precisely to use it asynchronously.[3]

For Balázs, therefore, the use of asynchrony was of particular value in the way
it permitted the symbolic or metaphorical use of sound.

Despite this, many contemporary film critics have mistakenly concluded
that the Soviet filmmakers, such as Eisenstein and Pudovkin, were against the
introduction of sound. Gianluca Sergi, for example, argues that:

> The position of most Russian formalists, such as Pudovkin and
> Eisenstein, helped reinforce a sense of distrust in sound ... They argued
> that sound reinstated an element of reality that potentially threatened
> their aesthetic and political project (the two being inextricably linked) ...
> the Russian school reinforced the notion of sound being a hindrance to
> the image – indeed, a threat to filmmaking aesthetics.[4]

In fact, as the manifesto quoted above indicates, the Soviet filmmakers were
not opposed to sound *per se* so much as its subordination to the picture. In
this respect, as Ian Christie argues, the early sound theorists were less involved
in resisting the use of sound than 'creative thinking' around the uses to which
it might be put.[5]

The concept of asynchronous sound has also been relatively neglected in
film scholarship. Asynchrony refers to a lack of synchrony or correspondence

2 Sergei Eisenstein, Vsevolod Pudovkin and Grigori Alexandrov in John Belton and Elisabeth
Weis (eds), *Film sound* (New York, 1985), p. 84. 3 Béla Balázs in Belton and Weis (eds), *Film
sound*, p. 120. 4 Sergi, *The Dolby era*, p. 59. 5 Ian Christie in Larry Sider, Diane Freeman and
Jerry Sider (eds), *Soundscape: the school of sound lectures, 1998–2001* (London, 2003), p. 169.

in time. In the cinema, asynchrony refers to the non-synchronous use of sound in relation to the visuals. Synchrony and asynchrony are different conceptually and are not to be mistaken with the more commonly discussed terms of diegetic and non-diegetic. Diegetic sound refers to both on and off-screen sound. Off-screen sound could mean a character is not seen but is still heard within the diegesis (talking from another room, for example). Non-diegetic sound refers to such elements as voice-over, narration and source music that can be heard by the audience but not by the characters within the film. Whereas diegesis relates to a sonic space, synchrony and asynchrony refers to temporal relationships between image and sound.

The complex way in which synchronous and asynchronous sound are used together in Lynch's films may be seen in *Eraserhead*. Thus, while an industrial wasteland is shown in an opening sequence of the film, the sounds associated with it continue throughout the film and rarely cease. In this way, the warehouses may not be shown again but the soundtrack asynchronously invests the domestic settings with a disturbing mood. There is a similar combination of synchronous and asynchronous sound in *The Elephant Man* except that, in this film, the opening shots of the film, involve asynchronous sound but are then repeated towards the end of the film with synchronous sound. In the opening scene, no clues are given to why the sounds of pistons are heard when elephants are seen on screen. Later in the film, after having been harassed by the night porter, the opening scene is replayed as John Merrick's nightmare. Merrick by this point in the film understands enough of the brutality existing in the world to be able to piece together what may have happened to his mother. In this way, the enigma created by the asynchronous relationship of the sound and image track in the opening sequence is answered towards the end of the film. In both *Eraserhead* and *The Elephant Man*, Lynch employs contradictory sound and visual elements to reinforce a sense of surrealism, and the workings of the unconscious mind, that is a hallmark of his work. This use of asynchrony to evoke a dark, dream-like reality may also be found in the opening sequence of *Blue Velvet*.

The film takes its title from the song of the same name and Bobby Vinton's version of it provides a good example of the way in which asynchronous non-diegetic music is used within the film. Lynch has explained the importance of the song for his film as follows:

> It was the song that sparked the movie! Bernie Wayne wrote the song in the early fifties. I forget who sung it first, but it wasn't Bobby Vinton. But Bobby Vinton's version was the first one I ever heard. I

don't know what it was about that song, because it wasn't the kind of music that I really liked. But there was something mysterious about it. It made me think about things.[6]

By using the song, the film seeks to evoke a different time. However, while the film relies upon a sense of another time, it does not transplant us to another period. The visuals locate the film in the present (1986) and the song is used to create an ambiguity about temporality that other elements within the film reinforce.

At the film's beginning, the camera tilts down from a blue sky onto a white picket fence, with red roses in front of it. In the audio mix, the sound of birds tweeting can be heard alongside the song 'Blue Velvet'. Both picture and sound create an idyllic suburban world. This shot dissolves from the roses to a shot of a man waving as he passes by on a fire engine. This is then followed by dissolves to yellow flowers in front of a white picket fence, a group of children crossing the road with the aid of a lollipop woman and an establishing shot of a house. None of these shots contains new diegetic sound; only the continuing song and the sound of the birds can be heard on the soundtrack. The film then cuts to a shot of a man watering his garden, which is accompanied by the sound of the water spraying from the hose mixed with the music. But, when the camera cuts inside the house to a woman watching television, the sounds of the television are strangely absent. The lack of diegetic synchronous sound here creates an imbalance in the soundtrack and places an increased interest in the man watering his garden, through the use of asynchronous non-diegetic sound.

Splet uses this disjuncture in the soundtrack to build tension. The sound of the increasing water pressure becomes more dominant in the mix. Although the music is still heard, the sound cutting continues in an abrupt manner and does not smoothly link one shot to another. The editing of images also consists of hard cuts, which contrast with the opening sequence of dissolves. These picture and sound cuts suggest that something bad is about to happen, and it does when the man is seen having a heart attack. However, as the man struggles on the ground, the music continues to play and the sound of the water coming out of the hose is also heard. The music could be considered asynchronous at this point, as the cheerful world the music conjures up is at odds with what is seen on screen. It is also unclear where the music is coming from. Is it source music or is it coming from the little brown box on the steps? If it is coming from the brown box/radio, then it would be diegetic sound. However, the song does not have the sound quality of music being played from a radio, or what is labelled 'worldized' sound in film terms.[7] 'Worldized'

6 David Lynch in Chris Rodley (ed.), *Lynch on Lynch* (London, 2005), p. 134.   7 Walter Murch in Michael Ondaatje, *The Conversations: Walter Murch and the art of editing film* (New York, 2003), p. 119.

refers to sound that has the acoustic qualities of the space in which it is occurring. So, in this case, the radio should sound like a radio, with a narrow bandwidth and perhaps a tinny quality due to the size of the speaker. These characteristics are not, however, present in the way the film uses the song. This was not, of course, a mistake by Lynch and Splet. They had been creating 'worldized' sounds since their first project together on *The Grandmother*. Rather, Lynch and Splet are deliberately confusing the issue of the sound source to disorientate the audience and create the sense of a disturbing, not quite explicable, universe within the film. They do this by blurring of lines between diegetic and non-diegetic sound, which in turn throws up questions as to whether the sound is synchronous or asynchronous with the picture.

A child and dog are then seen as the man struggles on the ground. The dog is seen in slow motion, but is heard barking in real time as he drinks from the jet of water. This makes the sound of his barking asynchronous to the picture. The tranquil sounds of birds and music give way in the mix as the camera proceeds to track through the grass. The cuts turn to dissolves but when the music eventually fades into the background Splet adds eerie sounds of the grass being pulled back. Splet then gets the soundtrack down to a momentary point of silence in order to make the sounds that follow all the more dramatic. Thus, when the camera enters the earth and the insects are seen scurrying underground, an ominous loud sound accompanies the picture. In a telephone interview, Ann Kroeber, the location sound recordist on the film (and Splet's wife), explained to me how these sounds were achieved using a FRAP contact mic which picks up sound as if it is within the sound itself. The sounds of mosquitoes in a beaker were also used to create an extra layer of soundscape to accompany the insects. In his discussion of sound, Michel Chion has coined the term 'synchresis' (a fusion of the words 'synchronism' and 'synthesis') to describe a synchronized sound effect that gives specific semantic weight to an image within the film.[8] In *Blue Velvet*, this fusion of sound and image could be described as 'hyper-syncretic' in the way in which normally inaudible insect sounds are heard at a heightened volume in order to suggest the disturbing currents just below the surface of small-town America. This is reinforced by the way the scene then cuts abruptly to a welcoming billboard for the town of Lumberton to the accompaniment of a radio station jingle. However, while there are tannoy speakers attached to the 'Welcome to Lumberton' sign, the omnipresent sound of the radio station throughout the town and woods is not realistic. Thus, while some of the early sound is 'worldized', and diegetically motivated, by the time the light jazz track is introduced, it is not.

8 Michel Chion, *Audio-Vision: sound on screen* trans. Claudia Gorbman (New York, 1994).

CONCLUSION

In a scene shortly after this, Jeffrey searches for a stone. The radio station or jazz track can no longer be heard and the sound again becomes eerie, mixing a bird's squawk, a distant chainsaw and some high frequency sound effects of a musical nature. The sound builds as Jeffrey discovers an ear covered in ants which he puts into a brown bag and walks off. The sound designer Randy Thom once said, '[f]ilms need to be given an ear', and here Lynch literally gives us an ear to interpret the film. The sound effects and sound design created by Splet not only provide narrative insight but also enhance the emotional qualities of the film. Operating both synchronously and asynchronously with the image, the soundtrack is able to complement as well as subvert the visuals. In doing so, Splet's use of sound becomes a key element of *Blue Velvet*'s complex, emotional journey into the dark and sinister underbelly of Middle America. Thus, while Lynch's films are commonly analysed in visual rather than aural terms, I have tried to indicate the importance of sound in the construction of meaning and therefore of the need for close attention to the soundtrack in film analysis.

Notes on contributors

DUDLEY ANDREW is Professor of Comparative Literature at Yale University where he also co-chairs the Film Studies Program. His books include *Mists of Regret: Culture and Sensibility in Classic French Film* (1995) and *Film in the Aura of Art* (1986).

AILEEN BLANEY was awarded a postgraduate scholarship from the Higher Education Authority's North-South Programme for Collaborative Research as administered by Film Studies, Trinity College Dublin, where she is based, and the School of Media and Performing Arts, University of Ulster. Her research is concerned with the representations of traumatic events in Northern Ireland's history from 'Bloody Sunday' to 'Omagh' and 'Holy Cross'.

CIARA CHAMBERS was awarded a postgraduate scholarship from the Higher Education Authority's North-South Programme for Collaborative Research as administered by Film Studies, Trinity College Dublin, and the School of Media and Performing Arts, University of Ulster, where she is based. Her research is concerned with the representation of the two parts of Ireland in film newsreels.

KEVIN CUNNANE was awarded a postgraduate scholarship from the Higher Education Authority's North-South Programme for Collaborative Research as administered by Film Studies, Trinity College Dublin, where he is based, and the School of Media and Performing Arts, University of Ulster. His research is concerned with the representations of Ireland north and south and their distribution and exhibition patterns in the country and abroad.

ALEXANDER FISHER is currently completing a PhD on 'Uses of Music in African Cinema' in the Centre for Media Research at the University of Ulster at Coleraine.

LIZ GREENE is currently completing a PhD on the use of sound in film in the Centre for Media Research at the University of Ulster at Coleraine.

JOHN HILL is Professor of Media at Royal Holloway, University of London, and Visiting Professor of Media Studies at the University of Ulster. His most recent book is *Cinema and Northern Ireland: Film, Culture and Politics* (2006).

MIKA KO is completing a PhD at the University of Ulster at Coleraine on the representation of 'otherness' in contemporary Japanese cinema and lectures in East-Asian Studies at the University of Sheffield.

NIAMH MCCOLE was awarded a PhD in 2005 at Dublin City University for her thesis, 'Seeing Sense: The Visual Culture of Provincial Ireland, 1896–1906'.

KEVIN ROCKETT is Associate Professor of Film Studies and Head of the School of Drama, Film & Music, Trinity College Dublin. His most recent book is *Irish Film Censorship: A Cultural Journey from Silent Cinema to Internet Pornography* (2004).

RASHMI SAWHNEY is completing a PhD at the University of Limerick. Her research is exploring the aesthetics of post-new-wave women's cinema in India.

JOHN DARA WALDRON was awarded a PhD from the University of Limerick in 2004.

PÁDRAIC WHYTE is an IRCHSS Government of Ireland Scholar, studying for a PhD at Trinity College Dublin. His research is examining film and literature for children in Ireland.

Index